THE KITCHEN HANDBOOK

AN ENVIRONMENTAL GUIDE

Pollution Probe recommends that The Green Shopper:

* Buys fresh, locally grown produce (that hasn't been shipped across the country).
* Cooks in-season fruits and vegetables (and cans them for use later in the year).
* Supports certified organic farmers (who don't use pesticides and other agricultural chemicals).
* Starts a backyard or balcony garden.
* Avoids overpackaged, convenience products.
* Eats low on the food chain (giving up meat at least once a week).

TERI DEGLER is the author of several books including *Scuttlebutt, Straight from the Horse's Mouth, Love, Limits, and Consequences: A Practical Approach to Kids and Discipline*, and *The Canadian Junior Green Guide*. She has an M.A. in special education and has been active in the environmental movement for many years.

POLLUTION PROBE was established in 1969 as an independent, non-profit, research-based charitable organization. Through memberships or donations, more than 90,000 Canadians are Pollution Probe Partners. Pollution Probe researchers/writers for *The Kitchen Handbook* are WILLIAM M. GLENN, an award-winning science writer and environmental consultant, and RANDEE L. HOLMES, a freelance writer and researcher who contributed to *The Canadian Green Consumer Guide, The Canadian Green Calendar 1991*, and *Profit from Pollution Prevention*. Teri, Randee, and Bill also collaborated on *The Canadian Junior Green Guide*.

ACKNOWLEDGEMENTS

Like *The Canadian Junior Green Guide* before it, this book was the result of an extremely successful team effort between author Teri Degler and Pollution Probe representatives William Glenn and Randee Holmes.

Teri Degler and Pollution Probe would like to thank Patricia Chilton, Janine Ferretti, Marcus Ginder, Ellen Schwartzel, Ellen Stevens, and Janet Sumner for providing their expertise. As well, they extend their thanks to Douglas Gibson, Linda Williams, and Mark Delvecchio of McClelland & Stewart, to designer Andrew Smith, and to editor Shaun Oakey. Teri Degler gives additional thanks to Gwen Campbell, who originally conceived the idea.

TECHNICAL DATA

The text of *The Kitchen Handbook* has been printed on Appollo Opaque stock, an acid-free paper. Appollo stock is made of 50% recycled fiber, of which 10% is post-consumer recycled. Recycled paper falls into two broad categories—secondary fiber and post-consumer. The former refers to those paper remnants that are created during the production process and reused at the mill. Post-consumer means a product has left the paper mill as newsprint, stationery, or another finished good, then been returned for recycling.

All inks used in the text are vegetable-based.

The majority of McClelland & Stewart's trade titles are now being published on recyclable acid-free paper. Virtually all paper used internally at the company's Toronto offices is being reused, with the exception of fax paper. Boxed shipments of books are being sent with non-CFC (chlorofluorocarbon) packing materials.

In October 1990, M&S instituted an in-house "Blue Box" program for the recycling and reuse of various kinds of paper waste. That same year the company became involved with Trees Ontario, a non-profit foundation established by the Ontario Forestry Association and the Ministry of Natural Resources to administer tree-planting and tree-tending programs in the province.

APPLIANCES

Many appliances are high-price items—and they have not one price tag but two. The first is the one you see in the store. The second is the price you will pay for the appliance's energy consumption over the years you own it. Since these energy costs can amount to more than the original cost of the appliance, it makes good economic sense to make energy efficiency a top consideration. And it makes even better environmental sense.

All of our traditional sources of energy come with high environmental costs. Coal-burning power plants that produce electricity are directly related to major pollution problems such as acid rain, global warming, and air pollution. Nuclear-generated power plants cause a different set of environmental problems, including the nightmare of long-term storage of radioactive waste and the threat of nuclear accidents such as the ones that occurred at Chernobyl, Three Mile Island, and Arco, Idaho. The huge water reservoirs needed for hydro-generated power contribute to the buildup of heavy metals in fish and in our waterways. Building hydroelectric plants always destroys habitat, sometimes for endangered or threatened species. Many of the plants currently planned in Canada will flood enormous areas of native lands.

It is clear that we need to make conserving electricity a high priority—whatever the source of our power.

Points to Consider When Choosing Appliances

REFRIGERATORS

Considering energy costs is particularly important when you are choosing a refrigerator: it consumes more energy than any other appliance in the home. In fact, the only thing that uses more energy than keeping your food cold is heating your entire house and supplying the large amounts of hot water most families use. Also, a fridge lasts an average of 17 years, and energy savings—or costs—can mount up over that time.

Buying Tips
★ *In general, refrigerators with side-by-side doors use the most energy, while those with one-door and manual-defrost use the least. (This can vary greatly with the type you buy.)*

HOW TO USE ENERGUIDE

The Energuide label tells you approximately how much electricity in kilowatt hours the appliance will use each month.

✳ Since everyone uses appliances differently, the amount of energy used will vary—but this does not mean Energuide ratings are meaningless (a ploy salespeople sometimes use!).

✳ Compare the Energuide ratings of several brands and models to see which is the most efficient.

✳ The lower the number, the more energy-efficient the appliance. An appliance with an Energuide rating of 50 kWh is twice as efficient as one with a rating of 100.

✳ You can calculate the approximate energy costs per month by multiplying the Energuide rating by the cost of a kilowatt hour of electricity. (Phone your local power company for this figure.)

Sample Energuide rating for two frost-free refrigerators in the 440 to 510 L (16 to 18 cu ft) range

* The most efficient fridge's Energuide rating: 73 kWh per month
* The least efficient fridge's Energuide rating: 145 kWh per month

Buying the fridge with the lowest rating would cost you about $808 more at today's energy prices over the lifetime of the appliance.

★ *Choose the right size for the number of people it will serve. Since a fridge lasts so long, consider how large your family might become.*

★ *It's better to choose one fridge with all the space you need than to put your old one in the basement and keep two on the go.*

★ *Fridges built before 1972 tend to use as much as 40% more energy than those built today. An old fridge that you keep around for a spare could cost you over $100 in energy a year.*

★ *Buy a refrigerator on wheels so you can roll it out at least every six months to vacuum the coils.*

★ *Measure the space for the fridge before you buy and make sure you have at least 1 in (2.5 cm) on each side for air flow.*

★ *A fridge with an energy-saver switch can save you money. Experiment to see which setting gives you the maximum energy savings* without *causing condensation on the outside of the unit. The right setting may vary with the seasons, so don't forget to adjust it.*

FREEZERS

Many people would never consider owning a freezer because they seem like such large, energy-guzzling appliances. Of course, the way you use your freezer can greatly affect energy consumption. When it is used for storing food that is grown at home in an organic garden or even for produce that is grown locally and bought in season, it *can* mean an overall energy savings. A large freezer that is not kept full—or one that is used to store highly processed foods and TV dinners—isn't doing anyone any good. If you use your freezer just to store overflow from the freezer unit in your fridge, operating the freezer will certainly be costing you money.

Buying Tips

★ *In general, chest freezers are far more energy-efficient than upright models. Cold air tends to stay in them better.*

★ *Chest freezers require defrosting only about once a year, so there's no need for a self-defrost function—an energy-eating option on many of the uprights.*

★ *Canadian manufacturers make some of the most efficient freezers in the world. But not all models are good, so shop around.*

★ *Purchase a freezer with a drain so you don't have to sponge up water after cleaning or defrosting.*

★ *Freezer size is an important consideration. Figure in no more than 4.5 cu ft (130 L) for each person.*

For more information on how to use and maintain your appliances so you save money and energy over the years, read Chapter Three.

COMBINED FREEZER/FRIDGE CAPACITY:

* for 1 to 2 people—12 cu ft (340 L)
* for 3 to 4 people—14 to 17 cu ft (395 to 480 L)
* for each additional person add 2 cu ft (55 L)

DISHWASHERS

Washing dishes by hand is generally more energy-efficient than using a dishwasher, especially if you wash a sink full of dishes without letting the water run for washing or rinsing. A great deal of energy and resources are used in making the dishwasher in the first place. Still, for many families, a dishwasher is a handy appliance and can result in the savings of some water and energy. Hand-washing dishes three times a day while letting the water run can use up about 25 gal (95 L) of water, while an energy-efficient dishwasher switched on once a day uses only about 16 gal (60 L).

Buying Tips
★ *Since about 80% of the energy a dishwasher uses goes to heat water, the most energy-efficient dishwashers are the ones that use the least water.*
★ *Some newer units have an extra-powerful spray action that cuts down on water use.*
★ *Compare Energuide ratings to find the most efficient brand.*
★ *Buy one with a switch that allows you to turn off the heat-drying cycle. Air-drying takes a little longer but works just as well and consumes no electricity. If your model doesn't have such a switch, simply unlatch the door at the start of the dry cycle.*
★ *Look for a dishwasher with a booster or "sani" heater that heats the water to the recommended 140° F (60° C) so you don't have to turn up your home water heater to this high temperature. Setting your water heater at 140° F is a big energy waste — 130° F (54° C) is hot enough for household use.*

RANGES

When shopping for a range—or a separate cook top and oven—you'll notice that the Energuide ratings don't differ as widely as they do for other appliances. Still, a stove is used so often that even a small energy savings can be significant in the long run.

And here's a bit of good news when you're thinking about housework: self-cleaning ovens can be as energy-efficient as the clean-it-yourself kind. Because they are better insulated than regular models, they tend to save enough energy in daily cooking to more than compensate for the high heat used by the self-cleaning function (if you don't use it more than two or three times a year).

CHECK IT OUT!
Before you make a major purchase, consult a consumer publication

✳ They test and rate thousands of products every year.

✳ They publish indexes to help you find articles on the product you want to purchase.

✳ Two highly recommended Canadian magazines are *Canadian Consumer* and *Protect Yourself*.

GAS RANGES
As a rule of thumb, natural gas is environmentally preferable to electricity. Many cooks also find gas stoves provide greater control over cooking temperature.

✳ Unfortunately, Energuide ratings do not apply to gas ranges.

✳ Look for a well built and well insulated gas range.

✳ Choose one with an electronic ignition rather than a continually burning pilot light:
  – you could use at least 30% less fuel
  – one estimate says 10% of *all* natural gas used goes to keep pilot lights burning!

Electricity vs natural gas

In a province like Ontario, where 75% of energy needs are supplied by "dirty" sources like coal and uranium, natural gas is a much cleaner alternative. Generally, if your area gets its electricity by burning fossil fuels or from nuclear-generated power plants, natural gas is a more environmentally sound choice. During combustion, natural gas produces fewer polluting emissions than other fossil fuels.

Buying Tips

★ *Conventional burners tend to be more energy-efficient than smooth-top models, although newer models are somewhat improved.*

★ *If you need an exhaust fan, choose one with a heat exchanger or one that meets your needs with minimum power-use. Some types can waste energy by sucking out a great deal of warm air in the winter and cool air in summer.*

★ *Purchase an oven with a window in the door so you don't let heat escape when you check the food.*

★ *Consider purchasing a range and oven that use natural gas.*

ENERGY-EFFICIENT ALTERNATIVES FOR COOKING

If you do a great deal of cooking, consider using the following energy-efficient alternatives. While many families continue to use a conventional oven some of the time, many are cutting down on energy costs by choosing these alternatives whenever they can.

Toaster ovens
- Heating a smaller space to cook small amounts of food saves energy.
- Be sure there is sufficient air circulation around the appliance, otherwise it won't work efficiently.

Microwave ovens
- A good microwave is the most energy-efficient type of oven.
- It cooks faster and can use half as much energy as a conventional oven since all the energy goes into heating the food itself, not the oven and pans as well.
- Unfortunately, Energuide ratings do not apply to microwaves.
- Be sure to allow for the recommended space for the air vents at the top, sides, and back.
- An optional temperature probe can shut the oven off automatically when the food is cooked.

Convection ovens
- Convection ovens have heating elements like the ones in conventional ovens, but they also have a fan that blows hot air around the food. This ensures more even cooking temperatures and results in a shorter cooking time at a lower temperature.
- Convection cooking is more energy-efficient than conventional but somewhat less efficient than a microwave.
- Countertop convection ovens are available, but both microwave ovens and regular ovens with convection features are more efficient.
- Beware: a poorly insulated countertop convection oven does not save any energy at all.

For More Information on Making Your Kitchen Environment-friendly

The Canadian Green Consumer Guide. Pollution Probe. Revised edition. Toronto: McClelland & Stewart, 1991.

The Healthy Home: An Attic-to-Basement Guide to Toxin-Free Living. Linda Mason Hunter. New York: Pocket Books, 1989.

The Healthy House: How to Buy One, How to Cure a "Sick" One, How to Build One. John Bower. Don Mills, ON: General Publishing, 1989.

Combination convection/microwave ovens

• A combination microwave/convection oven is more versatile and allows you to brown foods, unlike a microwave. It uses less energy than a convection oven but more than a microwave.

Other energy-savers

• *Slow cookers* are good for foods that require long cooking times. Cooking a stew in an oven takes twice as much energy as preparing one in a slow cooker, and although you use about the same energy preparing a stew on your stovetop, the slow cooker doesn't heat up your kitchen nearly as much. Slow cookers can save you money in another way: they make cheaper cuts of meat more tender. Choose the appliance size that fits your family's needs; slow cookers work most efficiently when they're at least three-quarters full. Also note that a continuous-heat model uses about 25% less energy than the ones that are thermostatically controlled.

• *Electric skillets* allow you to cook with less energy than you would on an electric stove when preparing small amounts of food.

Free Info on Energy Efficiency is available from:
Energy, Mines, and Resources Canada
Energy Publications
580 Booth Street
Ottawa, Ontario
K1A 0E4

SPICY SLOW COOKER BEANS AND RICE

This dish is particularly good served with corn bread or either corn or flour tortillas. Commercial chili powder along with a little cayenne and 1 to 2 cloves minced garlic can be substituted for the homemade chili powder but the results will not be nearly as flavorful.

1 lb	dried kidney beans, soaked overnight	500g
4 cups	water	1 L
2 tsp	salt	10mL
1	large onion, chopped	1
1	green pepper, chopped	1
2	(28 oz/796 mL) cans stewed tomatoes and liquid	2
1	4 oz (113 g) can green chilies, chopped	1
1–2 Tbsp	Homemade Chili Powder (recipe on page 53)	15–30 mL
2 cups	cooked rice	500 mL

1. Combine all ingredients, except the rice, in the slow cooker. Cover and cook on high for 2 hours. Turn the setting to low and cook for 8 to 10 hours.
2. During the last hour, add the rice and stir well.

Serves 4.

Do you really need an *electric*
can opener?
carving knife?
pepper mill?
pasta maker?
juicer?
knife sharpener?

- *Electric kettles* are more efficient for boiling water than a kettle on an electric stove *or* a microwave. Look for one with an automatic shut-off and a heat-resistant handle.
- *Electric coffee-makers* use less energy than making coffee on an electric stove.
- *Pressure cookers* are one of the most energy-efficient—and least appreciated—tools you can have in your kitchen. Foods cook two to three times faster than in a regular pot, with less water, and they maintain more flavor and nutritional value. Slow cookers are safe and simple to use. A consumer magazine, *Protect Yourself,* gives an excellent rating to the stainless steel T-Fal Sensor and a very good rating to the stainless steel Presto Express.

WATER AND LIGHTING

Water Conservation

Canadians use more water per capita than anyone in the world—except the Americans—and we're using more all the time. We are already taking almost as much water as possible from some of our rivers, especially in the southern prairies, and we are pushing many of our sewage treatment facilities beyond their capacity. Building ever-larger sewage treatment plants is expensive, and it eats up tax dollars that could be better used to prevent water pollution or restore damaged waterways.

Treating used water so we can safely send it back into the water system or reuse it takes energy. Pouring more and more water down our drains and sewers also increases the amount of contaminants, like chlorine, that enter our rivers and lakes.

Canadian water bills are about $16 a month, but this doesn't reflect the *real* cost of maintaining municipal water supplies and sewage systems. Environment Canada estimates that these costs may rise to as high as $8 to $10 billion over the next decade. This staggering figure doesn't even include the cost of supplying sewage treatment systems to the millions of Canadians who live in municipalities such as Victoria and Halifax, which don't even have them yet!

Lighting

Whether you are renovating your kitchen or making a few minor modifications, don't forget to consider the lighting. Good lighting is essential if you want to make your kitchen a place where you enjoy spending time. Since natural light is clean and free, the ideal green kitchen has several large windows.

Artificial lighting now uses about 1000 kWh per year—about 2% of the energy used in an average home—but new types of bulbs can reduce that amount by 70% to 80%. Multiply that sav-

CUT DOWN ON THE WATER YOU WASTE IN THE KITCHEN!

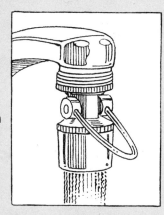

* If you use a dishwasher, run it only when it's full, and use the "econo" cycle.
* If you wash dishes by hand, wash and rinse in a partly filled sink or basin; never leave the water running. Washing dishes from one meal can use up 9 to 14 gal (40 to 60 L) of hot water.
* Wash vegetables the same way, then rinse or spray them quickly. Letting the water run can waste 5 to 6 gal (20 to 40 L) a minute!
* Fill a kettle only with as much water as you need.
* Cook vegetables in as little water as possible. Use a tight-fitting lid. This saves both nutrients and water. Steamers, pressure cookers, and microwaves are great for this.
* Don't run water to cool it for drinking. Instead, keep a jug ready in your fridge.
* Turn taps off tightly and fix leaks immediately. A leaky tap can send 8 gal (30 L) of water down the drain every day.
* A "low-flow" faucet can decrease your water usage by 25%—or more depending on the product—with no perceptible decrease in water pressure.
* Remember: if you're wasting hot water, you're also wasting the money and energy it took to heat it!

ing by all the homes in North America and you have an energy saving that makes a difference.

The key to choosing energy-efficient lighting is in understanding the difference between watts and lumens. Watts measure the amount of electricity a lightbulb consumes; lumens measure the amount of light the bulb puts out. The type of bulb you choose can make a huge difference in the number of lumens you get per watt consumed. Though some of the more energy-efficient bulbs cost a good deal more than the incandescents we normally use, they can more than pay for themselves in energy savings and length of life.

Fluorescent bulbs are clear winners in the energy-savings department. They also last far longer. A fluorescent tube, for instance, uses one-fifth to one-third the electricity used by an incandescent that produces the same amount of brightness, and it will last 10 to 20 times longer.

Compact fluorescent bulbs produce a quality of light that is just the same as that of incandescents— no more buzzing, flickering, or blue cast with these bulbs. The quietest bulbs have an A rating. Some models even screw into standard fixtures; for others, adapters are available.

BULB BURN-OUT

If your bulbs seem to be dying an unnatural death by burning out long before the package says they should, there may be a good reason:

* Excessive vibration, even the type caused by children running and jumping in the house, can shorten a bulb's life expectancy. Try bulbs designed for "rough service."
* Excessive voltage causes bulbs to burn out quickly. Some homes are supplied with voltage somewhat higher than the standard 120 volts. An increase of just 10 volts can shorten a bulb's life by one-third. Have your power company check it out; they may be able to regulate the voltage. Otherwise look for bulbs rated for 130 volts in an electrical-supply store.

Type of bulb		Number of lumens per watt of energy consumed	Hours of life
Incandescent		14–18	750–1000
Long-life incandescent		10	2500
Tungsten-halogen		20	4000
Fluorescent		40–80	10,000

A tungsten-halogen bulb, a type of incandescent, may use only as much power as a regular bulb, but it lasts up to 6000 hours longer, and it doesn't darken with age. (This darkening causes conventional bulbs to gradually lose 10% to 15% of their brightness over their lifetime.) It contains a small tungsten filament surrounded by a halogen-filled quartz crystal, similar to a car's headlight.

Task Lighting for Your Kitchen

Task lighting—illuminating specific work areas—is becoming increasingly popular in kitchens. It's particularly efficient because it eliminates the excessive ceiling light that is often used in a vain attempt to brighten the areas where the measuring, mixing, chopping, and washing are done.

Task lighting shines directly on the work area, so your own shadow doesn't blot out the light. Fluorescent strip lighting, attached beneath wall cupboards or shelves, works extremely well.

Lighting Hints
★ *Place task lighting so that the light shines on the work and not in your eyes. Sometimes a shade or diffuser is the answer.*
★ *Paint your kitchen a light colour. White walls and ceiling reflect 80% of the light that shines on them. Black, on the other hand, absorbs all but 10% of the light.*
★ *Keep in mind that 90% of the energy used by an incandescent bulb is dissipated in heat—something you don't need in the summer.*
★ *If you do use incandescent bulbs, note that one 100-watt bulb gives off one and a half times as much light as four 25-watt bulbs.*
★ *Long-life incandescents last longer but give off 10% to 15% less light per watt used.*
★ *Put your incandescent fixtures on a dimmer switch so you use that high wattage only when you need it.*
★ *Put fluorescent fixtures on separate switches to give you more lighting flexibility.*

One fluorescent can save you the cost of nine incandescent bulbs plus $31.50 in energy costs over five years.

COOKWARE

Choosing cookware carefully is important for many reasons. First, you want pots and pans that will last for a long time. As we mentioned, North Americans' tendency to overconsume and throw things away is wreaking environmental havoc. An exceptionally good set of pots and pans will last for decades, if not a lifetime or longer. An equally important consideration, however, is how well pots and pans work. Cheap cookware tends to conduct heat poorly. If you cook, you know how easy it is to burn something in a pan that doesn't heat up evenly—and you probably know how hard it is to get a child to eat a scorched pancake. Since burnt food is wasted food, it makes good environmental sense to choose cookware that allows you to cook well.

The most expensive cookware is not always the best. Compare before you buy, and make sure you're not being charged just for a fancy design or pattern that adds nothing to the quality of the cookware.

Most pots and pans are made of metal, and of course environmental concerns surround the production of all metals. For this reason, some environmentalists choose glass or ceramic cookware, but these, too, come with an environmental price. Until studies prove conclusively which materials are the hardest on the environment, it makes sense to pick cookware that will cook well—that is, conduct heat evenly—and last a very long time. And, as always, it makes good environmental sense to take care of what you have, use it for as long as possible, and resist the temptation to buy new cookware just because it's trendy.

Aluminum
- Pans made of thick aluminum—not the thin, cheap stuff—are winners in the heat-conducting category. The heat spreads evenly along the bottom and up the sides to make cooking more efficient.
- Thin to medium-gauge aluminum pans tend to warp, which results in poor cooking efficiency and wasted energy as little of the bottom of the pan comes in contact with the heating element.
- Aluminum is light-weight and doesn't rust, but alkaline foods like broccoli can stain it. Remove these unattractive marks by boiling a solution of vinegar and water in the pan.
- A tiny amount of aluminum may leach into food, especially when you're cooking salty or acidic foods. These types of foods should never be stored in aluminum pans.

Anodized Aluminum
- While the possible link between aluminum cookware and health problems such as Alzheimer's disease is still being hotly debated,

it is certain that many foods naturally contain far more aluminum than ever leaches from properly used aluminum cookware.

- Still, some people now prefer to use a product called anodized aluminum that is said to prevent leaching.
- Anodized aluminum has the added advantage of being scratch-resistant and relatively non-sticky.
- It is designed—unlike regular aluminum—not to react with acidic foods or to be stained by alkaline foods.

Stainless Steel

- Stainless steel is an alloy of iron, chromium, and nickel; it sometimes contains other metals such as molybdenum or titanium.
- It's tough, long-lasting, and resistant to corrosion and tarnish.
- It is not a good heat conductor, so foods tend to stick in spots and burn. Choose cookware that has a thick aluminum or copper bottom.
- Acidic or salty foods can cause surface pitting if stored in stainless steel pots and pans.

TO SEASON A CAST IRON PAN...

Wash it, dry it well, rub it down with a good deal of oil or unsalted fat, and place it in a slow oven (250 to 300° F/120 to 150° C) for about three hours. Wipe out the excess grease and cool. Cook with your cast iron carefully, so you don't get a burned-on crust. After use, wash it out lightly, and dry it thoroughly. Don't wash it in the dishwasher. If you ever scrub your cast iron pan, you'll have to season it again. Many cooks store their cast iron pans in the oven rather than the cupboard because they are always coated with a light film of oil.

Cast Iron

- There's nothing like cast iron for giving foods a crispy, crunchy coating. Some cooks use nothing else.
- Foods cooked in this material contain more nutrient iron, but it is not known if our bodies can absorb the mineral in this form.
- A properly treated and seasoned cast iron pan is almost as non-stick as one with a commercial non-stick coating.
- Well-cared-for cast iron cookware can last for generations.
- On the negative side, cast iron tends to be very heavy and somewhat brittle, and it is not the best conductor of heat. Acidic foods may react with it.

Copper

- Copper is an exceptionally good heat conductor, but it is expensive and easily damaged, so it is best suited for the professional cook.
- Cooking acidic foods in copper will cause the metal to be released right into the food, and although copper is an essential nutrient, too much can cause illness.
- Copper cookware is often lined with tin or stainless steel, which eventually wears through and has to be professionally replaced.
- Unlined copper is for decorative use only. Antique copper pots may make exquisite kitchen ornaments, but don't cook with them; they may well have been soldered with lead.
- Copper requires frequent polishing to keep it looking good. Use a paste of salt and vinegar or lemon juice instead of a commercial cleaner.

Glass, Ceramic, and Enamel

- Glass cookware is extremely popular with some cooks, though some feel it doesn't conduct heat as well as metals. It doesn't react with food and it doesn't stain, and overall it's probably a good environmental choice.
- Cookware coated with porcelain enamel is stain- and scratch-resistant. It is safe: lead is not used in the glaze. But some sources recommend replacing utensils as soon as the enamel begins to wear through.
- To lengthen the life of enameled cookware, don't heat it or cool it too rapidly, and avoid steel-wool pads and abrasive cleaners.

THE MICROWAVE CONTROVERSY

Most people agree that a properly used microwave oven can be a real energy-saver. For this reason, we generally recommend their use. However, some people still have concerns about the microwave, even though government regulating agencies consider them quite safe. These concerns include:

* The interaction in the microwave between food and its packaging.

* Two products that appear to break down during the microwaving process are heat-susceptor packages—the kind used to make pizza crisp—and polyvinyl chloride (PVC) plastic wrap.

* It also seems that furans and dioxins, both toxins, might migrate from paper microwavable trays to the food.

* Radiation leakage from the microwave door when the door seals wear down or when the door seals are cracked open by bits of food or paper.

* Microwaves as a source of potentially harmful non-ionizing radiation—or electro-magnetic fields.

CHECK FOR LEAD!

A number of kits are now available to help you check for lead in such things as the glaze on that brightly colored dinnerware that comes from countries with lower safety standards. Lead is also found in the glazes of some ceramic pots used in slow cookers. Even though U.S. tests claim the level of lead from these slow cookers is quite safe, you might prefer to choose one with no lead.

Another source of lead is food cans imported from countries where the lead soldering of cans is still allowed. These cans have a thick, dark strip running down the seam. You might want to test one you think is lead, and then you'll be able to avoid that type in the future. Canadian food cans are no longer soldered with lead; they are welded or extruded.

Lead test kits are available in some health food stores or can be ordered through ads in some health and environmental magazines.

Non-stick Coatings

- The old standby non-stick coating, Teflon, and the newer Silverstone are essentially made of the same material; Silverstone has three layers of it.
- Little information is available on the actual environmental impact of producing the coating, which is perfluorocarbon resin, a type of plastic.
- Still, this cookware can make for efficient cooking and reduce food waste caused by sticking and burning in regular pans. It can also be cleaned easily without soap pads or harsh cleaners, and good brands can be long-lasting and durable.
- Early concern about whether swallowing tiny bits of the coating was harmful seems to have been allayed by FDA studies that showed the plastic resin to be inert—it will not chemically combine with food and if a little bit was swallowed it should pass right through your body.
- However, caution is called for! Temperatures higher than 500° F (260° C) can cause the material to break down; temperatures over 600° F (315° C) can result in the emission of irritating fumes that can cause flu-like symptoms.
- Most domestic cooking does not exceed 450° F (230° C)—but never allow a pan with a non-stick coating to overheat. One consumer magazine warns against using them for broiling. As with all pans, they should never be left unattended when in use.

Waterless Cookware

- Stainless steel waterless cookware is just becoming popular, so it's hard to say how good it will prove over the long term. But it certainly sounds ideal.
- Vacuum-sealed, this cookware uses no water and cooks at low temperatures, so it saves water and energy. Estimates for British Columbia say that using waterless cookware three times a day could save cooks $110 a year!
- Some brands have carbon steel transfers that carry heat up the sides. Six to eight pots can be stacked one on top of the other with as little as a three-degree temperature difference between the top and bottom pots.

CHAPTER TWO
STOCKING YOUR SHELVES

The choices you make when you buy groceries represent one of the most powerful tools you have for encouraging environmental change. Every time you reach for a product you vote with your shopping dollars. You can choose to support local farmers who are trying to make a living, or you can support multinational agribusiness. You can advocate organic farming practices or those that require the dumping of billions of tons of pesticides on Earth each year. You can decide to support farms where livestock is raised in humane ways or factory farms where animals may be raised in undesirable conditions and routinely be given drugs. You can underwrite companies that deliver environment-friendly products in reasonable packaging or those that waste energy and resources creating overpackaged, heavily processed goods.

What you spend your shopping dollars on in North America even has an effect on the ruination of lands, the spread of famine, and the living conditions of people in developing countries.

These are sobering thoughts. The issues that revolve around food are not simple—and they are never easy to deal with. In this chapter—however disturbing some of the information may be—we hope to give you a sense of the tremendous power you have as a consumer and to remind you that you do have a choice, you do have a vote. If we all stop buying certain products, food producers will eventually make changes. Consider the influence people like you recently had on the tuna industry. In 1990 environmental organizations began publicizing the plight of dolphins that were being needlessly slaughtered in the nets of some tuna fishermen. A boycott was quickly organized, and within a year three of the major tuna companies had stopped buying tuna from any fishing fleets that routinely killed dolphins. Today, the dolphin-friendly logo is a common sight on the labels of canned tuna.

CHOOSING ENVIRONMENT-FRIENDLY GOODS

Although many of the issues surrounding food production are complex, choosing environment-friendly foods is fairly simple. There are basically four things to consider:
• Where and when was it grown?
• How was it grown?
• How did it affect the environment?
• How is it packaged?

SHOPPING FOR A BETTER WORLD

A small book called *Shopping for a Better World* (by the Council on Economic Priorities, Bantam Books, 1991) is an indispensable tool for wielding influence with your shopping dollars. The book rates performance in 10 major areas of concern including the environment, animal testing, the advancement of women and minorities, and charitable donations. Notations inform you if the company is involved in other areas, for instance the development of armaments or the production of Salvadorian coffee.

This wonderful guide makes no judgments; it simply provides you with the information and lets you decide which issues you want to take a stand on. It is well organized, handy, and easy to use. You can find it in many health food stores and bookstores.

Support Companies That Offer *Solutions!*

An increasing number of products help the environment. The snack Rainforest Crunch, for example, is made from rainforest nuts gathered by peasants. Selling the nuts provides them with money for food, so they no longer have to cut down trees to create farmland.

Buying Locally and in Season

"Bioregionalism" is a term that is becoming well known. It describes a movement to buy locally grown, in-season produce and, specifically, to support local farmers.

Bioregionalism makes good sense. First, tremendous quantities of fossil fuels are used to transport food. Think of the energy needed to truck strawberries from California to Toronto or to ship kiwi fruit from New Zealand to San Francisco. In fact, carting one five-calorie strawberry from California to Toronto uses up about 435 calories of fossil fuel energy!

Second, fresh fruits and vegetables from afar are often not really fresh. Chemicals, wax, and questionable storage procedures may all be used to create the illusion of freshness. Tomatoes, for instance, are picked green because they are still hard and will travel without bruising. They are then packaged and shipped, often thousands of miles, to their destination. There they may be "gassed" with an ethylene spray that turns them red. And we wonder why the tomatoes we buy in winter don't taste like tomatoes!

Third, fruits and vegetables imported from other countries may have been treated with pesticides whose use has been banned here in North America. Ironically, some of these chemicals are still produced in the United States and Canada and sold to countries with less stringent pesticide laws. They can then come back to haunt us on imported fruits and vegetables.

Although produce coming into the United States and Canada is supposed to be tested for banned chemicals, the volume of imports is too great for any useful amount of testing to be done. In Canada, limited funding and personnel allow for the testing of less than 1% of all imported food. Per capita, the United States spends far less and has far fewer personnel doing the same job.

Finally, it makes sense to support family farms. They can often produce a quality of product that the megafarms simply cannot match, and according to some sources, the family farm can produce food more cheaply than the megafarms can.

> *The sooner you begin buying more organic produce, the sooner the prices will be more competitive.*

Buying Organic

Eating organically grown food and supporting organic farmers is not just good for you, it's good for Earth. Conventional farming practices are the major source of the pesticides that are poisoning the planet. These pesticides run off into rivers and pollute lakes, oceans, fish, and drinking water. They also kill off valuable species of insects and soil organisms as well as birds and other creatures.

Pesticide use isn't the only questionable practice on conventional farms, particularly the megafarms. Farmers once relied—and some still do—on rotating crops, letting soil lie fallow once every few years, or planting nutrient-rich crops and then plowing them under to replenish the soil. Today's megafarms don't have time for allowing land to lie fallow or for planting and plowing under. They are also usually dependent on marketing one specific crop, so they don't want to rotate crops. Because they don't use the time-proven methods to replace what they have taken out of the soil, they have to rely on ever-increasing quantities of synthetic fertilizers and pesticides: as the soil becomes depleted, the yield decreases and becomes more susceptible to disease, and the greater the farmer's dependency on chemicals. The depletion of nutrients from the soil can also contribute to the erosion of precious topsoil.

Many conventional farmers are, of course, concerned about the environment. But they are caught in a system that makes it difficult for them to make a living without modern hybrid seeds, pesticides, and fertilizers. They also have to contend with the fact that we, the consumers, demand perfectly formed, unmarked produce from them. Still, an increasing number of conventional farmers are experimenting with less harmful forms of pest control and are going back to traditional methods such as crop rotation.

HOW TO BE SURE IT'S ORGANIC

You often have to pay a little more for organic produce, and you want to be sure it really was organically grown. So look for the label on the produce or nearby sign that says "Certified Organic."

* This label means the produce has been certified by one of the organic certification programs.

* Although standards differ, certification usually means that no pesticides or synthetic fertilizers were used on the labeled produce, and none were used on the farm for at least three years.

* These farms must submit to regular soil tests to check for pesticides.

* Certified organic farms are also committed to soil enrichment.

* The label "transitional organic" means the farm is becoming organic but is still in the three-year transition period; these farms deserve your support too.

* The label "natural" means only that the product contains no synthetic ingredients; for example, refined white sugar can be called "natural."

These farmers need to be supported in their efforts. Fortunately, when we follow the concept of bioregionalism and buy locally grown food, many of these farmers receive our support.

When we buy organically grown foods, we take a far more active stand against questionable farming practices. On "certified organic" farms no pesticides or synthetic fertilizers are used. Organic farmers are committed to soil enrichment rather than soil "mining"; that is, they use traditional methods like composting and crop rotation to put back into the soil what they have taken out.

As the demand for organically grown food increases, more organic farms will be able to survive economically, and more conventional farmers will be able to switch to organic methods.

What to Ask Yourself Before You Buy

* *Was the produce grown organically?*
* *Was the meat or poultry raised free-range?*
* *Is the food close to its natural state or has it been heavily processed?*

Getting Organic Food Into Your Supermarket

While there's a lot to be said for supporting your local health food store by buying your produce there, you will also be helping organic farmers if you campaign to make organic produce available in your local supermarket. In the long run you'll also save yourself money. The sooner buying organic becomes widespread, the sooner organic food prices will become completely competitive. Here are three ways you can help:

* Next time you're in your supermarket, ask to talk to the produce manager. Tell the manager of your concern about pesticides, and say you would prefer to buy certified organic food and that you'll go elsewhere if you can't get it from this store.
* Write to the head of your supermarket chain and tell him or her the same thing. If you know of supermarkets that do offer organic produce, mention them!
* Encourage your friends and family to do the same.

THE LITTLE-BITTY SEED IN WHOSE HANDS?

A frightening trend is the development of fertilizer-dependent seeds. These strains of seed are hybrids, often developed by the fertilizer and pesticide companies themselves to produce higher-yielding crops. But these strains will grow only if they are treated with a specific set of chemicals—naturally, those that are sold by the company that developed the strain in the first place. In this way, the chemical companies increase our farmers' dependence on their products.

Even worse, as more of these hybrid strains are developed—and owned—by the chemical companies, an increasing number of natural seed strains fall out of use. They eventually become extinct.

When several different strains of a crop are grown across an area, the entire crop is not likely to be wiped out by one particular disease, since different strains are naturally resistant to different diseases. There are fears that our growing dependency on a few strains of seed could lead to massive crop destruction in the event of disease epidemics.

A few seed banks or museums exist to preserve the many natural varieties of seeds. But they are often privately run and in serious need of funding. If you know of one, support it. And stop indirectly supporting the chemical companies—buy from organic farmers!

ANOTHER BALL OF WAX

Waxes are used to enhance the color of and preserve a number of fruits and vegetables and to make consumers think they are getting a fresh product when in fact they are not.

✳ You cannot always tell by looking whether produce has been waxed.

✳ Most waxes do not wash off. They have to be peeled off, and they may be present on products like green peppers that are not easily peeled.

✳ Some waxes may contain fungicides.

✳ Locally grown, in-season produce is less likely to be waxed.

✳ Produce labeled "organic" is unlikely to be waxed unless it has been shipped a long way.

✳ U.S. grocers are required by law to label waxed produce, but nobody seems to bother. In Canada there is no such regulation.

Common Waxes
Carnauba wax comes from the wax palm in Brazil.
Paraffin is a petroleum derivative.
Candelilla is made from a reed.
Shellac comes from the bodies of a female scale insect.
Polyethylene is a plastic made from petroleum.
Oleic acid can come from vegetable oils, animal fats, or petroleum.
Tallow comes from animal fat.
Waxing can be said to have some benefits: it keeps some foods fresh-looking longer and prevents some spoilage. But we should have the right to choose—and we can't do that unless grocers begin labeling waxed produce. Lobby your government to make and enforce regulations!

Some
Often-Waxed
Fruits and
Vegetables
Apples
Cucumbers
Lemons
Eggplants
Limes
Parsnips
Oranges
Peppers
Passion fruit
Rutabagas
Sweet potatoes
Pineapples
Squash
Melons
Tomatoes

	Apples	Apricots	Asparagus	Beans	Beets	Blueberries	Broccoli	Brussels sprouts	Cabbage	Cantaloupes	Carrots	Cauliflower	Celery	Cherries	Corn (sweet)	Cranberries	Cucumbers	Eggplant	Endive	Fiddleheads	Garlic	Grapes (table)
Jan	G				G				G		G								G			
Feb	G				G				G		G								G			
Mar	G								G		G								G			
Apr	G								G		G							G				
May	G		G						G		G							G		G		
Jun	G		G				G		L		L							G		G		
Jul	L	G	G	G	G	G	G		L		L	G		L	G		L	G				
Aug	L	G		G	G	G	G	G	G	G	G	G	L	G	G		G	G			G	L
Sep	G			G	G		G	G	G	L	G	G			G	G	G	G	G		G	G
Oct	G			L	G		G	G	G	L	G	G	L		L	G	L	L	G		G	G
Nov	G				G		G	G	G		G	G				L			G			L
Dec	G				G				G		G					G			G			

FRUITS/VEGETABLES IN SEASON
Check your grocery store for local produce

■ PEAK	▨ GOOD	░ LOW	□ NOT AVAILABLE

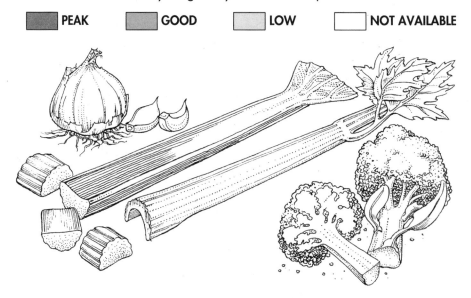

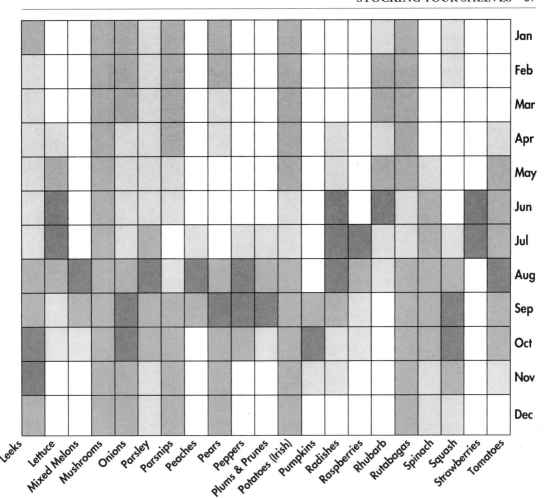

Leeks | Lettuce | Mixed Melons | Mushrooms | Onions | Parsley | Parsnips | Peaches | Pears | Peppers | Plums & Prunes | Potatoes (Irish) | Pumpkins | Radishes | Raspberries | Rhubarb | Rutabagas | Spinach | Squash | Strawberries | Tomatoes

How Fresh Is Fresh?

North Americans are one of the world's biggest consumers of fresh vegetables. An average American eats about 250 lb (110 kg) of fresh veggies a year, and the average Canadian puts away a whopping 500 lb (225 kg) of them. But how fresh are they? Not fresh at all, if they are not in season or locally grown.

Many nutritionists say produce that was canned or frozen soon after picking is as nutritious as—or even *more* nutritious than—"fresh" produce that has traveled long distances or been stored for more than a few days. To stock the green kitchen, and ensure your family gets the best nutrition, here's a list of choices.

* Buy locally grown, in-season organic produce.

* Buy locally grown, in-season produce even if you can't find organic.

* Buy from farmers' markets whenever you can, making sure the produce you buy really is locally grown.

* Grow your own organic produce and freeze or can it yourself.

* Buy large quantities of local produce in season and freeze or can it yourself.

* Remember that food frozen or canned locally can be a nutritionally and environmentally sound alternative when little locally grown, in-season produce is available.

Choosing Between Family Farms and Factory Farms

When we think of animals on farms we tend to picture chickens scratching in barnyards, horses frisking through the meadows, and cows grazing contentedly in fields of hay as they might have done in days gone by. While few animals on modern-day farms live in such idyllic conditions, they are generally well cared for. Farmers will tell you it doesn't make sense for them to mistreat their animals. Their livestock is, after all, their livelihood.

However, there is a trend in the United States, and to a much lesser extent in Canada, to create megafarms that are run and owned by agribusinesses rather than by individuals or families.

Most of these megafarms have been mechanized and streamlined to maximize productivity and profit. In itself this is not necessarily a bad thing. However, on some megafarms little or no consideration is given to the humane treatment of animals. Such farms have been dubbed "factory farms."

In some factory farms animals are always kept indoors, often in crowded conditions. A report in the *Utne Reader* (September/October 1988) describes factory farms where laying hens are kept in row upon row of cages about the size of a microwave oven—four hens to a cage. On some factory poultry farms the layers are tricked into laying eggs twice a day— instead of once as they naturally would—by manipulating the artificial light so that two day/night cycles are created every twenty-four hours. Layers on factory farms have a lifespan of about 18 months; barnyard layers might live for years.

The issue of animal treatment aside, the biggest concern about factory farms is the amount of drugs used. The conditions on many factory farms make them ideal places for the spread of disease. To prevent this, factory farmers routinely give antibiotics to *all* animals—not only those that are sick. According to Dr. Mitchell Cohen, deputy director of the bacterial diseases division of the Centers for Disease Control, this widespread use of antibiotics results in antibiotic residues in the meat and dairy products that humans consume. We do not yet know what long-term effects this might have.

According to Dr. Cohen and other scientists, it is probable that this overuse of antibiotics is contributing to the development of antibiotic-resistant strains of bacteria. There is particular concern about bacteria that cause food poisoning like salmonella, a potentially fatal bacteria that is reportedly found in as many as a third of the chickens eaten in North America.

The Centers for Disease Control states that reported cases of salmonella poisoning have increased sixfold in the past twenty-five years and that forty times more strains of tetracycline-resistant

---

Fight the Trend Toward Factory Farms

* Ask your grocers what type of farms the meat and poultry they sell is raised on. If they don't know, ask them to find out.

* Write to the head office and ask for information. Tell them your concerns.

* Support grocers and butchers who get their supplies from farmers who do not use factory-farming techniques.

* Buy products raised on small local farms.

* Buy meat and poultry products labeled "free-range."

salmonella now exist. In the March 5, 1987, *New England Journal of Medicine*, a group of doctors reported on their research and concluded that there was a direct link between the development of these antibiotic-resistant salmonella and the use of antibiotics in the diets of animals raised for food.

As consumers we can oppose the trend toward factory farming by choosing to buy products only from local individual- and family-owned farms. We can also look for the "free-range" label on meat and dairy products. Although this label does not guarantee that the animals were fed organically grown feed, it should indicate animals that were raised in fairly natural conditions, for instance cattle that grazed on a range and chickens that lived in barnyards.

THE CLOSER TO NATURAL, THE BETTER

As a general rule, you can assume that the closer a food is to its natural state, the better it is for you and the better it is for the environment. It has long been known that processing foods can remove or destroy valuable nutrients. Flour is a classic example. Whole-wheat flour has close to 30% more protein than white flour and two to three times as many vitamins and minerals.

Processing foods can be just as hard on the environment as it is on our health. Some food processing is, of course, worse than others; technically speaking, even freezing or canning vegetables is a form of processing. As mentioned earlier, although these processes have their environmental costs, they can still be reasonable choices—especially when done at home. In general, when

---

THE RISE OF AGRIBUSINESS

* Huge food corporations, or agribusinesses, are controlling more and more food production around the world. According to *The Supermarket Tour*, some authorities predict the entire world food market will be dominated by no more than 20 companies by the end of the century!

* Many agribusinesses are involved in almost all aspects of the food production: food processing and distribution, seeds, chemicals, plant and animal genetics (bioengineering), and veterinary medicine.

* Agribusinesses are particularly active in food processing. For example, five companies already control over half the world market in each of the common types of processing. In some processing areas the percentages are even higher: five companies control 87.5% of the breakfast cereal market, and four companies control 82.6% of the soft-drink market.

* Choosing to support small local farmers and choosing *not* to buy processed foods are two ways to remove your support from agribusinesses.

Animal Victories

* In 1987, the Swedish government announced a decision to ban factory farming. They are phasing out battery cages on poultry farms, eliminating the tethering of pigs, and guaranteeing the right of cows to graze outdoors.

* In 1990, the British government outlawed the use of veal crates. It is now a punishable offense in the U.K. to keep a calf in a single pen unless it can easily turn around in it. The calf must also be provided with adequate dietary fiber and iron.

we speak of processed and highly processed foods in this book, we mean the kind of processing that significantly alters a food, for instance turning a potato into instant mashed potato flakes or a healthful grain into a cereal called something like Sugar Crunchies.

The high processing of foods has three strikes against it. First, it requires tremendous amounts of energy to carry out the various processes involved. How ironic that we use up one precious resource, our fossil fuels, to strip the goodness from another, our food!

Second, highly processed food often contains numerous additives and preservatives. And don't forget sugar and salt! Both are frequently added to processed foods, even those with the tricky label "all natural." Sugar, a food with its own set of environmental problems, is added not just to encourage children to eat more of the product but also to increase bulk and weight. It is far cheaper for manufacturers to fill a product with sugar than with "real" food.

The third strike against processed foods is their packaging. By their very nature processed foods require packaging of some kind: an orange, for example, comes naturally wrapped, but orange-flavored fruity-roll-ups need cellophane and a box. Processed foods also tend to be *over*packaged. They often come in boxes that are plastic-coated, shrink-wrapped, or foil-lined. Each individual serving may then come in a plastic tray or be wrapped in foil, plastic, or waxed paper. Some of the worst examples of overpackaging are found in convenience foods like boil-in-a-bag or microwave-ready dinners. They often have four or five layers of packaging!

Packaging—A Bad Wrap All Around

✳ Packaging makes up as much as one-third of our garbage. The creation of packaging is related to the overlogging of forests, the depletion of fossil fuels, and the pollution caused by the pulp and paper and plastic industries.

✳ Packaging is used to manipulate us. It often convinces us of quality that isn't there and tricks us into thinking we're getting more than we are. Packaging on produce keeps us from judging freshness and often forces us to buy more than we need.

✳ Recycling is good, but reduction and reuse are better.

✳ Unneeded packaging is, in short, a totally unnecessary environmental waste. Let manufacturers know you won't put up with it any more.
  – Make products with *no* packaging your first choice.
  – Buy in bulk and take your own containers and bags.
  – Buy large-volume containers whenever possible and pour contents into handy small containers at home.
  – Choose products in refillable or reusable containers.
  – Look for products in packaging made from recycled materials.
  – Choose products in easily recyclable packaging.
  – Write to manufacturers of your favorite products and ask them to start providing large-volume containers.

GREENSPEAK OR REALLY GREEN?

Five minutes of watching TV commercials will tell you that "green" is in. As soon as marketing studies revealed that consumers wanted environment-friendly products, advertisers jumped noisily onto the bandwagon and began to trumpet how wonderful their products were for Mother Earth. Recently, the Canadian government has written guidelines for several common environmental claims and is hoping for volunteer compliance. If this compliance is not forthcoming, Consumer and Corporate Affairs has promised to pass appropriate legislation in the future. In the meantime consumers still need to exercise caution when considering a product with environmental claims:

* Use your common sense. Beware of claims that make you think you can maintain a lifestyle based on consumerism and yet "save the earth" by buying products that represent only a marginal improvement.
* Recognize that green advertising claims are simply marketing tools.
* Read *everything* on the label, then weigh what you read against what you know.
* Remember that one environment-friendly aspect, for example a recyclable container, does not mean the product isn't harmful at some stage in its manufacture, use, or disposal.
* Keep informed so you can read labels intelligently.

Here are a number of common environmental labels and some of the ways they are frequently—but not always—used:

ORGANIC

Organic means that the product is made out of the building blocks of life: hydrogen, carbon, and oxygen. Anything that is or was once living is organic. Theoretically, anything labeled organic should contain *only* organic matter and the elements that occur naturally in the product's growth. There should be no synthetic ingredients or residues.

CERTIFIED ORGANICALLY GROWN

Certified Organically Grown has not yet been defined by government regulations; however, independent regulating bodies such as the Organic Food Producers Association of North America have established guidelines for using the label on produce and meat and dairy products. The produce has been grown on land that has been free from all synthetic fertilizers and pesticides for at least three years and only natural alternatives have been used to increase yields and control pests and weeds. The meat and dairy products come from animals that have been fed only organically grown feeds, have been raised under conditions of minimal stress, and have not been given growth-enhancing hormones or been routinely given antibiotics to prevent illness.

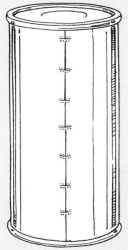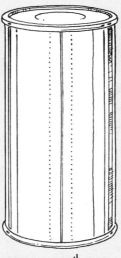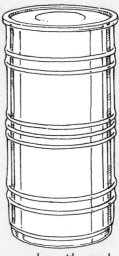

wide, thick, sometimes
dented seam contains lead

narrow smooth seam
is lead-free

seamless with round
bottom is lead-free

Free-Range is another label that is still open to interpretation. Ideally it should be used for meat and dairy products that come from animals that were raised under conditions of minimal stress and given access to fields or barnyards as appropriate.

Natural means only that the product contains no synthetic (man-made) ingredients. For example, white sugar can be labeled "all natural" even though it is highly processed and usually comes from sugarcane or sugar beets that were not organically grown.

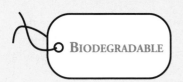

Biodegradable should mean that the product will break down into water, carbon dioxide, and/or non-toxic carbonaceous soil and nothing else. Ideally—as the California legislature has recently decreed—biodegradable products should also break down within a year in the environment wherethey are most likely to be disposed of. *Degradable* means simply that the material will break down into extremely small particles. Degradable plastics, for example, break down into a fine dust—but it is still plastic dust.

CFC-Free means the product, usually aerosol sprays or polystyrene plates and cups, contains no chlorofluorocarbons—the compounds infamous for causing holes in the ozone layer. Such products are also labeled "ozone-friendly." Although some aerosol cans carry one of these labels and others do not, *all* aerosol cans in Canada are now CFC-free. The CFCs in many aerosol products and in some polystyrene products have now been replaced with compounds known as HCFCs. HCFCs cause about 75% less damage to the ozone than CFCs do—but they still cause damage. It is far better to choose refillable pump-spray containers and reusable plates and cups.

CFCs are still being used in refrigerator and air-conditioner coolants, in some cushion, mattress, and carpet underlay foams, and in some types of home insulation.

Phosphate-Free now appears on a number of laundry and dish detergents and fertilizers. Phosphates are harmful once they are washed into rivers and streams, because they act as a fertilizer and cause vast amounts of algae to grow. Unfortunately, recent studies indicate that some phosphate-free laundry detergents contain surfactants—the compounds that agitate the dirt and lift it into the water and keep it from settling back into your clothes—that may agitate the heavy metals polluting many of our waterways, making them more potentially harmful. This means your best choices are pure soap and washing soda for the washing machine and the organic compounds often found in health food stores for the dishwasher. If you insist on using commercial detergents, the current rule of thumb is: If you live in an area where untreated sewage flows directly into the waterways, choose phosphate-free detergents; if you live in an area with good sewage treatment facilities, choosing detergents with some phosphates may be less harmful than using those that are labeled "phosphate-free."

Recyclable means simply that a product or, more commonly, its packaging can be recycled. The term is meaningless, however, unless the product can be recycled in your local recycling program *and* you intend to recycle it.

CONTAINS
RECYCLED MATERIAL

THIS ITEM CAN
BE RECYCLED

ECOLOGO

CONVENIENCE FOODS—HOW CONVENIENT ARE THEY?

Next time you're tempted to buy a convenience food to save time and effort, consider how much time you're really going to save. A boxed macaroni and cheese dinner doesn't save you anything but grating the cheese. The only difference between making muffins from a mix and from scratch may be adding your own baking powder and salt.

There are alternatives to so-called convenience foods. What about getting the kids to help? While they might not show a lot of enthusiasm for shelling peas, they're generally more than happy to help with cookies and desserts. And preparing meals with your kids or your partner is a great way to get in more of that quality time.

Another option is to make double and triple amounts each time you cook. Freeze the extra, and you've made your own convenience food!

How Foods Affect the Environment

When we're rushing down the crowded aisles of a supermarket, we're usually trying to figure out the best buys or struggling to remember what was on the list we forgot to bring. Considering the environmental impact of food is probably the last thing on our minds. Yet it is one of the most important considerations when we're stocking our green shelves. And although the environmental effect of food is a complex subject, there are a few simple guidelines to help you make environmentally sound choices.

First, consider how interconnected everything is on the planet; it's a notion that is easy to forget in our highly mechanized society. Few of us think about the Brazilian palm tree that was destroyed to provide us with tiny, tasty hearts of palm or about the peasants in Kenya who receive 69 cents a day to harvest our coffee. Most of us would just as soon *not* think about these things. However, we *must* begin to understand that the choices we make in the supermarket have implications for the condition of the environment and the conditions in which people live around the world.

PROTECT YOUR HEALTH

Eating low on the food chain is good for environmental and health reasons. Toxic chemicals such as pesticides tend to concentrate in animals that are higher on the food chain. This occurs because many animals, cattle for example, need to eat several pounds of plant food to develop a pound of flesh. Although some non-organically grown plant foods do contain more pesticides than some animal products, we still need to be particularly wary of those pesticides that concentrate—or "bioaccumulate"—in animal

> As a rule of thumb, chemicals tend to concentrate in fat. Thus, if you choose to eat animal products, you can decrease your chance of consuming chemicals by buying leaner cuts and trimming off fat and skin. Low-fat and skim milk and milk products are also healthier than whole-milk products.

Support Food Co-operatives
Food co-ops are a great way to purchase foods in bulk, avoid supermarket chains, and provide you with organically grown goods at reasonable prices. They are essential in areas where no adequate natural food stores exist. For more information on food co-operatives, see Chapter Eight. For more information on co-operatives of all kinds, write:

The Canadian
Co-operative
Association
275 Bank Street
Suite 400
Ottawa, Ontario
K2P 2L6

The National
Co-operative
Business Association
1401 New York
Avenue NW
Suite 1100
Washington, D.C.
20005-2160

flesh: if they concentrate in the flesh of other animals, they probably concentrate in ours. After all, we are animals, too.

Most chemicals found in meat products come from pesticides sprayed on feed crops, and the antibiotics being overused on factory farms can be passed on to consumers. As well, some farms treat hogs and cattle with hormones to increase growth. According to Agriculture Canada, growth hormones in livestock pose no threat to meat consumers and they may be used legally with a veterinarian's prescription. They are, though, expensive and are probably only being used in experimental programs. Little is known currently about whether eating "second-hand hormones" affects humans.

THE FOOD CHAIN

There has been a lot of talk lately about eating low on the food chain, but unless you're a long-time vegetarian or have read one of the classic books on the subject, you may not have been exposed to exactly what this means.

Although we generally talk about *the* food chain, there are, in fact, many food chains in nature. A food chain consists of a number of plants and animals, each one consumed by the next—and higher—one on the list. All food chains begin with small, simple plants like algae and grass; at the other end are complex animals like humans, hawks, and sharks. For instance, plankton, a single-celled green plant, floats in the sea; a small fish eats the plankton; a larger fish eats the little fish; a bear eats the fish; a hunter shoots the bear and eats it.

The distinctive thing about humans is that we can choose where we want to eat on the food chain. We eat low on the chain when we eat plant foods, including fruit, vegetables, legumes, and grains. We eat high on the chain when we eat animals (meat). We are eating especially high on the chain if we eat a creature like a large fish, a bear, or a shark that has consumed meat already. The higher we eat on the food chain, the greater the number of plants and/or animals that have been consumed, both directly and indirectly, to create the food we eat.

Some industrial pollutants also tend to accumulate in animal products. A Canadian study found dioxins and furans, two common carcinogenic by-products of incineration, in a number of foods. The highest concentrations were found in meat and dairy products.

Scientific evidence also tells us that increasing the amount of plant food in our diet is good for our health. Among other things, it decreases the amount of fat we consume and increases the amount of fiber—both changes that more and more doctors are advocating as preventive medicine.

PROTECT THE ENVIRONMENT

Health concerns and questions aside, eating low on the food chain is good for the environment. Frances Moore Lappé brought one of the primary reasons for this to public attention in her book *Diet for a Small Planet.* She writes that when beef cattle are raised in a feedlot system it takes 16 lb (7.25 kg) of grain to put 1 lb (0.5 kg) of beef on our table. That amount of grain, if eaten directly by humans, could provide eight times the protein and 21 times the calories with only three and a half times the fat that the beef provides. Hogs and other farm animals are big grain consumers, too.

Some estimates on the amount of grain consumed to produce beef are much lower than Lappé's. For instance, Agriculture Canada currently provides the following statistics. The beef in this case is primarily range-fed and then fattened in a feedlot to improve its tenderness and flavor.

Amount of grain and soy consumed	To produce 1 lb (500 g)
5 lb (2.3 kg)	beef
6 lb (2.7 kg)	pork
3 lb (1.4 kg)	eggs
2 lb (0.9 kg)	chicken

The grain, soy, and other feeds consumed by livestock in the United States alone is approaching 200 million tons a year. This represents about one-half of the harvested acreage in the country. Planting, watering, fertilizing, spraying with pesticides, and harvesting this vast amount of cropland has enormous environmental implications. The fossil fuel used to grow 1 lb (0.5 kg) of feedlot-fed beef would grow about 40 lb (18 kg) of soybeans. In fact, according to a joint Departments of the Interior and Commerce report quoted by Lappé, "one-third of the value of *all* raw materials consumed for all purposes in the United States is consumed in livestock foods."

Massive amounts of fertilizers and pesticides are used on feed crops. Corn producers in the United States use some 30 million tons of toxic chemicals annually just to control one pest, the corn

> **COSMIC COINCIDENCE?**
> The foods that are best for you tend to be the same ones that are best for the environment.

borer. And the majority of corn grown in the United States is destined for livestock.

Livestock also consume about 15 gal (57 L) of water a head *each day*, while it takes only 25 gal (95L) to raise a pound (500g) of wheat. Livestock waste contributes to water pollution too. According to Douglass Lea in *Mother Earth News*, 90% of water pollution from organic sources in the United States comes from livestock. And livestock need a lot of space. An acre of land can be used to grow 20,000 lb (9000 kg) of potatoes—or 165 lb (75 kg) of beef.

> "Our daily choices about food connect us to a worldwide economic system. Even an apparently small change—consciously choosing a diet that is good both for our bodies and for the earth—can lead to a series of choices that transform our whole lives."
>
> *Frances Moore Lappé*

ON THE OTHER SIDE OF THE FENCE

After considering the facts given in this chapter about livestock production, it's easy to see why so many environmentalists are urging people to reduce their consumption of meat and eat at least one meatless meal a week. Yet there are no easy solutions to these complicated issues. Meat and dairy producers have their side of the story, too:

✳ Cows and some other livestock are quite efficient at turning something we can't eat, like grass, into something we can eat, like milk.

✳ Much of the grain produced to feed livestock is a lower standard than that grown for humans.

✳ A great many cattle graze on marginal land that cannot be cultivated for crops.

✳ Livestock are killed not just for their meat. Almost every part of a cow is used: bones for gelatine and glue, intestine lining for sausage casings, hair for artists' paintbrushes, and much more.

✳ Important pharmaceuticals are made from livestock by-products. For instance, some insulin is obtained from cow pancreases, and corticotropin, a drug used to treat respiratory diseases and leukemia, comes from cow pituitary glands.

It is also worth noting that until the 1950s most cattle went straight from the range to the slaughterhouse. Today, cattle are either raised exclusively in the feedlot or are taken off the range and fattened or "finished" in the feedlot for up to four months. Beef producers tell us they *have* to do this because consumers don't like the taste of range beef.

Respecting both sides of the story, here are some options:

✳ Let cattle growers know you are willing to eat beef that has never seen a feedlot. After all, people were happy with it for centuries.

✳ Buy free-range meat and poultry products; they have at least been raised humanely. The beef should be primarily grass-fed.

✳ Buy organically raised meat and poultry products. If all farmers fed livestock only untreated feeds, the use of pesticides in North America would be drastically reduced.

✳ Make meat a supplement in some meals instead of the main ingredient.

✳ Eat at least one meatless meal a week, or try cutting your meat consumption by about 10%. According to *Mother Earth News*, a 10% reduction in the fossil fuels used to produce meat would mean the U.S. would no longer have to import oil!

Fish

Fish, high in protein and generally low in fat, is considered one of the healthiest foods you can eat. However, water pollution—industrial waste, oil spills, untreated sewage, garbage, agricultural run-off, and the dumping of radioactive waste—is taking its toll on fish both by reducing their numbers and by making them less safe to eat.

* Learn which species are likely to have high residues and don't eat them more than once a month.

* Fatty fish such as carp, catfish, white perch, and mackerel tend to have the highest concentrations of residues.

* Offshore species tend to have the least residues. Cod, haddock, flounder, pollock, salmon, and shrimp have little.

* Before you buy fish, ask where it was caught; avoid fish from highly populated or industrial areas.

* Broil, bake, or poach fish. Don't use the drippings or poaching water.

* Trim away the fattiest tissue—skin, belly flap, and dark meat—after cooking.

* Don't eat a lot of raw fish, and avoid raw shellfish.

* Buy tuna canned in water rather than oil, and rinse it before using.

* Keep in mind that fish farming creates waste that runs off into our waterways; it may include chemicals, herbicides, and drugs.

Buy only
dolphin-friendly
tuna!

CASH CROPS AND OTHER COUNTRIES

Cash crops are grown, as the name implies, to supply money rather than food or a balanced diet to the people who grow them. The issues that surround cash crops in developing countries are extremely complex, and although it is impossible to explore them thoroughly in a book that is not dedicated to the subject, we need to provide you with an overview, for cash crops have far-reaching implications for the people and the environment in developing countries.

Some of the most common cash crops are cotton, coffee, tea, sugar, bananas, pineapples, and peanuts. In many cases, cash crops were introduced into a country by individuals who saw a chance to make a great deal of money. Before the cash crops were introduced, the people often lived in a natural harmony with the land, growing what they needed to feed their families quite adequately and practicing age-old farming methods that returned nutrients to the soil, prevented erosion, and left the land able to survive drought.

THE CASH CROP CYCLE

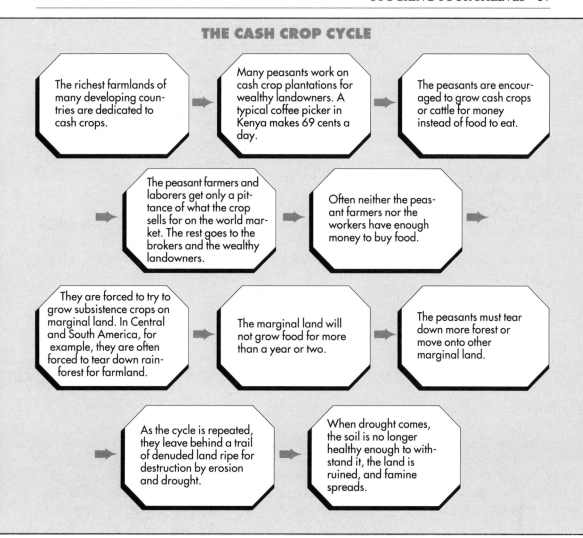

The richest farmlands of many developing countries are dedicated to cash crops.

Many peasants work on cash crop plantations for wealthy landowners. A typical coffee picker in Kenya makes 69 cents a day.

The peasants are encouraged to grow cash crops or cattle for money instead of food to eat.

The peasant farmers and laborers get only a pittance of what the crop sells for on the world market. The rest goes to the brokers and the wealthy landowners.

Often neither the peasant farmers nor the workers have enough money to buy food.

They are forced to try to grow subsistence crops on marginal land. In Central and South America, for example, they are often forced to tear down rainforest for farmland.

The marginal land will not grow food for more than a year or two.

The peasants must tear down more forest or move onto other marginal land.

As the cycle is repeated, they leave behind a trail of denuded land ripe for destruction by erosion and drought.

When drought comes, the soil is no longer healthy enough to withstand it, the land is ruined, and famine spreads.

The Peanut and African Famine

The story of the peanut in Africa's Sahel region shows graphically how cash crop farming can result in denuded soil, erosion, and the spread of famine. In his book *The Real Cost*, Richard North reports that the growing of peanuts was promoted by loans and subsidies from French authorities and business interests in the Sahel in the 1950s. In Nigeria, land that was once used for subsistence farming and land that had previously been allowed to lie fallow were both planted with peanuts. Although some French colonial authorities saw the danger of this and tried to stop it, within a few years half the area's farmers were dependent on peanuts for half to three-quarters of their income. Other farmers were less but still heavily dependent.

Peanuts are a crop that strip the soil rapidly of nutrients. Worse yet, the farmers in the Sahel had been sold improved-yield seeds, which were more heavily fertilizer-dependent than normal peanuts. As the farmers became increasingly dependent on selling peanuts

For more information on how food issues affect the environment and developing countries, read:

The Real Cost.
Richard North.
London: Chatto &
Windus, 1986.

Food for Beginners.
Susan George and
Nigel Paige.
London: Writers and
Readers Publishing
Cooperative Society,
1982.

to buy the food they had once grown themselves, they could no longer afford to let any land lie fallow. They were forced to go deeper and deeper into debt to buy ever-increasing amounts of fertilizer. As well, the peanut farms put an end to the traditional yearly nomadic movement of cattle and herders from the north to the south of Nigeria. This meant the cattle no longer came to deposit their enriching dung on the land.

By the 1960s France was cutting back on the subsidies and financial support that had created the peanut farms. Farmers were forced to expand to meet costs. The expansion moved into lands the nomadic cattle herders needed for moving their cattle. The cattle were forced onto marginal lands that they soon stripped of vegetation. The land the peanuts were grown on was becoming poorer and less able to withstand erosion and drought. When the natural cycle of drought—which the peasants were once prepared for—came, the land was too poor to withstand it. Widespread famine ensued.

The French are certainly not being singled out here. Every developed nation has played similar roles in many countries. Coffee, for example, is the most valuable trading commodity in the world next to oil. It is grown exclusively in poor southern countries—but four-fifths of it is drunk in the rich northern ones.

HOW TO REACH ALTERNATIVE TRADERS

Although most alternative traders have outlets only in major cities, several have mail-order catalogues.

Bridgehead
Oxfam Canada
20 James Street
Ottawa, Ontario
K2P 0T6

Oxfam America
PO Box 821
Lewiston, ME 04240

Self Help Crafts
704 Main Street
Box L
Akron, PA 17501

Support Alternative Traders

Supporting alternative traders is one of the most powerful ways you can work for social change. These traders are individuals and organizations from developed countries who are dedicated to forming fair trading partnerships with people in developing countries. Many of them benefit the environment indirectly by promoting sustainable development and trying to break the destructive cycle created by current cash crop practices. Among other things, members of the International Federation for Alternative Trade:

• Buy products from small, independent producers or democratically organized producer groups where all participants are ensured a fair wage.

• Try to work with groups that not only generate income but also have a positive social outlook.

• Try to buy directly from the source so that brokers are eliminated.

• Sell the products to people in developed countries at a price that is fair but that ensures a fair wage to the producer.

• Provide information so people in developed countries are aware of how unfair trading practices affect the poor and oppressed people in developing countries.

LOW-ON-THE-FOOD-CHAIN FOODS FROM AROUND THE WORLD

Long ago, when Mexicans first ate beans and corn tortillas together and Middle Easterners first dipped pita into hummus, people had never heard of protein. And they had certainly never heard of combining incomplete proteins to form complete ones. They found that these were the foods that kept them healthy, and so eventually these food groupings became central to their cuisine.

Almost all of the world's cultures have traditional staple dishes that use legumes, grains, and rice to their best advantage. The recipes in this section all have ingredients that work well together: chickpeas, pita, and the sesame in tahini; beans and corn; pasta and cheese. They represent the scores of intriguing food combinations that will make your adventure along the food chain so eye-opening—and delicious.

Homemade Curry and Chili Powders

These homemade mixes save you money and have more flavor than commercial brands. They can be made in large amounts and stored, or can be whipped up quickly for a recipe. The amount of each spice or herb can be varied to taste—especially for making curries. No one curry powder exists in India; curries are made of many different combinations of spices, but the following are often the key ingredients.

Curry Powder

2 parts	each ground coriander, cumin, turmeric, and garam masala*
1 part	cayenne pepper

* Garam masala is an Indian spice that can be found in Indian or specialty food stores. Although it is an important ingredient, you can leave it out and still make a powder that is better than many commercial products.

Chili Powder

3 parts	each coriander, cumin, and oregano
1–2 parts	cayenne pepper
2–3 parts	garlic powder (or add equivalent amount of fresh garlic to recipe when using)
Pinch	ground cloves per 2–3 Tbsp (25–50 mL) mixture

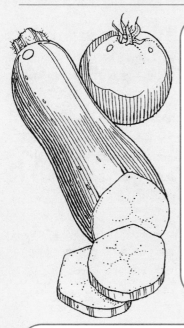

Eileen's Quick Zucchini and Tomato Pasta

This recipe is so delicious, you'll wonder why you ever spent hours making spaghetti sauce — but you must be sure to use only fresh ingredients.

2 Tbsp	cooking oil	25 mL
2–3	large cloves garlic, finely chopped	2–3
1	large green pepper, chopped	1
2–3	medium zucchinis, sliced thinly	2–3
	Salt and pepper to taste	
2–3	fresh ripe tomatoes, finely chopped	2–3

Teri's Beans and Corn Tortillas

Beans

3 cups	dried kidney or pinto beans	750 mL
8 cups	water	2 L
1	whole onion, peeled	1
1–2 tsp	cumin	5–10 mL
1–2 tsp	coriander	5–10 mL
1–2 tsp	oregano	5–10 mL
1 tsp	cayenne pepper	5 mL
Pinch	ground cloves	Pinch
1–2	cloves garlic, chopped	1–2
	Salt to taste	
	Tortillas (recipe follows)	
	Chopped onions and tomatoes, shredded lettuce, grated cheese, and salsa for garnish	

1. Discard old beans and any impurities. Wash well. If you are not using a pressure cooker, soak the beans overnight.
2. Drain the beans. Place all ingredients in large cooking pot. The amounts of the spices can be varied to taste. The quantities listed make a "medium-hot" dish. If these spices are not available, substitute with chili powder.
3. Cook beans until soft.Remove the onion. Salt to taste.
4. The beans may be served as they are or "refried" — either partially or thoroughly mashed and fried quickly in hot oil in a heavy skillet.
5. Place a scoop of beans in a folded tortilla and garnish.

Serves 4. Any leftover beans may be frozen or refried and used within 2 or 3 days.

1 Tbsp	oregano	15 mL
	Spaghetti cooked	
	al dente for 4	
	Grated mozzarella and	
	Parmesan cheese for garnish	

1. Heat cooking oil in a large frypan or wok, and sauté garlic and green peppers until just partially tender.
2. Add zucchini. Stir gently and cook until partially tender.
3. Add salt and pepper to taste.
4. Add tomatoes and oregano; simmer 10 to 15 minutes, stirring occasionally. (If the mixture isn't juicy, add a little water.)
5. Add cooked, drained spaghetti and toss well. Serve immediately, sprinkled with grated cheeses.

Serves 4.

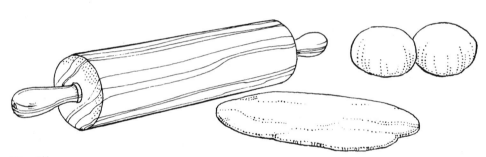

Tortillas

2 cups	masa (Mexican	500 mL
	corn tortilla flour)	
1 cup	warm water	250 mL plus 25 mL
plus 1 oz		

1. In a large bowl, mix together well the masa and most of the water.
2. Knead the mixture until all the masa is moistened and forms easily into a ball. The consistency of the mixture is very important. Add a little more water if the dough, after it is well mixed, seems to crack or does not stick together properly. The ball must be just wet enough to stick together — and no wetter.
3. Cover the bowl with a damp cotton cloth and set aside for about 30 minutes. (If you are using "instant" masa, skip this step.)
4. Using a rolling, patting motion of your hands, form the dough into 14 to 16 balls. As you work, place the finished balls to one side in the bowl and keep them, along with the rest of the dough, covered with the damp cloth.
5. Place the balls between squares of wax paper and flatten them into circles with a rolling pin or a tortilla press.
6. Cook each tortilla on a hot ungreased (or very lightly greased) griddle for about 30 to 45 seconds on each side.

The By the Way Café Falafel

2 1/2 cups	dried chickpeas, soaked overnight	625 mL
1 tsp	ground coriander seeds or powder	5 mL
1 tsp	ground cumin	5 mL
1/2 tsp	cayenne pepper	2 mL
1/2 tsp	salt	2 mL
1	clove garlic, crushed	1
1/4 cup	flour	50 mL
1 1/2	medium onions, finely minced	1 1/2
1/2 cup	freshly ground parsley Oil for deep-frying Pitas Green vegetables, tomatoes, and tahini for garnish	125 mL

1. Drain chickpeas and grind until coarsely ground in a blender or food processor.
2. Add coriander, cumin, cayenne pepper, salt and garlic; mix thoroughly.
3. Add the flour, onion, and parsley and mix thoroughly into a dough.
Form the dough into 1 1/4-inch (3-cm) balls.
4. Pour oil for deep-frying into a deep saucepan and heat to 375° F (190° C).
5. Deep-fry the falafel, a few at a time, for about 2 or 3 minutes or until they are golden brown.
6. Place two or three falafels in half a pita, garnish, and serve.

The By the Way Café is well known for its falafel. Run by Ruth and Amir Benedikt, the café is a landmark near Toronto's university district.

CHAPTER THREE
USING THE GREEN KITCHEN

The way you use your kitchen equipment and prepare your food goes hand in hand with how you stock your shelves in creating a truly green kitchen. You can spend a great deal of money on an energy-efficient fridge, but you cancel out the good you've done if you stand there with the door wide open while you leisurely decide what to have for supper. On the other hand, you may not have the money to buy a new energy-efficient stove, but you can do a lot to conserve energy by simple things like putting pots on burners that match their size. In other words, awareness and attitude are the keys to using your kitchen wisely.

As you have been reading through this book, you have probably noticed a recurrent theme: the real environmental cost of the things we buy and the food we eat is almost never reflected in the price.

Once we become aware of this fact, our attitude begins to change. We value things more. We begin to appreciate why so many people who have lived through depressions and wars feel that waste is such a crime. Attitudes in others that we once thought were a little silly no longer seem to be: we no longer tease our grandmother when she carefully washes a piece of tin foil so she can use it again and again.

In short, we realize the tremendous importance of conserving and of taking care. And when this happens, the way we do hundreds of little things begins to change. We no longer leave the kettle boiling away while we chat on the phone. When we're finished running water, we quickly turn it off. We find ourselves looking up recipes that will give us an idea for using the leftover rice in the fridge. When we see someone throw a pop can in the garbage instead of the recycling bin, we're a little bit appalled. Changes like these are signs that we are beginning to appreciate the real value—and cost—of what we have.

This chapter contains scores of ideas for using your kitchen equipment wisely and preparing food that is easy on the environment. As you adopt them you'll not only be helping planet Earth, you'll find yourself saving a considerable amount of money.

KEEPING YOUR KITCHEN GREEN

Despite their tractors, threshers, combines, and electric milking machines, farmers use far less energy growing our food than we do preparing it. Unfortunately, a lot of the energy we use to prepare food is wasted energy. A simple thing like cooking with a lid, for instance, prevents excess heat loss and decreases cooking time. Much of what we can do to make our kitchens and our cooking more environment-friendly are just as easy. One of the first things to consider is how to care for and use appliances so their energy efficiency is always at a peak.

Stovetops and Ovens

Except for continuously running appliances such as the fridge, our cooking ranges are generally our most often used kitchen appliances. The way we use them can make a major difference in the amount of energy we consume.

HINTS FOR USING RANGES

★ Today's ovens don't need to be preheated—unless you're baking pastries, cakes, soufflés, etc., and then 10 minutes of preheating is usually plenty.

★ Make the most of your oven heat. Once it's on, cook the whole meal in it, or cook something for a future meal.

★ You can cook several items in the oven at once if there's no more than 50° F (10° C) difference in their required temperatures. Set the oven on the average temperature and take dishes out when they're done.

★ Try not to open that oven door! As much as 25% of the heat can escape each time. Using a timer can help you omit some unnecessary door openings.

★ If you have a powerful built-in exhaust fan on your cooktop, use it only when you really need it. It sucks out a great deal of hot air in the winter and cool air in the summer.

★ Keep the drip pans under the burners clean, but don't use foil. It can reflect too much heat and damage the element.

★ Cooking frozen foods can use up to 30% more energy. Thaw them out first!

★ When you use heat-treated glass or ceramic pots and pans, set your oven 25° F (10 to 15° C) lower than what is suggested in your recipe.

★ Turn your electric oven off 15 minutes before roasts and casseroles are done—the oven heat will finish the job.

Tips for Gas Ranges

✳ An efficiently burning pilot light has a clear blue flame; a yellowish one needs an adjustment. Read your owner's manual for instructions.

✳ If you see flames licking the edges of your pan, you have your flame far too high.

✳ An efficiently burning cooking flame is a bright, clear blue. If you aren't getting this color, the gas jets may be clogged. Read your owner's manual for instructions.

✳ Any yellow or orange in the flame means it's too high. You're wasting gas and probably getting a lot of black on the bottom of your pans. Simply turn down the gas.

★ Insert steel nails—or the special "baking" nails found in kitchen stores—through the middle of potatoes and squashes to decrease baking time by 25% to 50%.

★ Clean up spills right after each use and you'll rarely need to use your oven's self-cleaning feature. When you do use it, do so right after cooking something to take advantage of the heat that's already generated. If you self-clean more than two or three times a year, you will probably cancel out the energy savings you get from the stove's extra insulation.

★ Save energy by setting your pan on the right sized element. The pan should just cover the burner.

★ Use tightly fitting lids for stovetop cooking.

★ Use as little water as possible in stovetop cooking.

★ Use high heat only to bring foods to the steaming stage. Immediately turn the heat down to the lowest temperature needed to cook the food.

★ After water boils turn the heat down to simmer. Lightly boiling water is the same temperature as water that's in a rolling boil.

★ You can often turn off an electric burner several minutes before the required cooking time is reached. The burners stay hot for a long time.

> ### WHAT COOKS QUICKER?
> Does food bake more quickly in glass than metal? Indeed it does, in part because glass is transparent. Radiant heat can pass directly through it, so it absorbs less heat, leaving more of the heat to cook the food. If some of your recipes don't seem to be timed correctly, they may have been tested in a different type of pan than the one you're using. When using oven-proof glass:
>
> ✳ For a recipe that works with a dark-surfaced pan, shorten the cooking time or lower the oven temperature by 10° F (5° C).
>
> ✳ For a recipe that works with a shiny pan you can decrease the oven temperature by as much as 25° F (15° C).

ALTERNATIVES TO USING THE RANGE

Always use the smallest appliance appropriate to the job. In deciding which appliance *is* the appropriate one, remember that toaster ovens don't cook efficiently when they're too full, and the more food you put in your microwave, the longer it takes to cook. Appliance instruction manuals often have just the information you need.

Toaster ovens
• Toaster ovens are efficient only for cooking small amounts of food.
• There should be plenty of room for the heat to circulate around the food.
• Check your instruction book for recommendations—and use your oven or microwave for amounts that are too large.
• Make sure surfaces used for reflecting heat within the oven are kept shining and clean. If they're dirty, they can't reflect.

Electric kettles
• Electric kettles use about half the energy that's used by boiling water on an electric stove.
• Fill the kettle only with the amount of water you'll need. That way, you won't waste energy boiling unused water.
• Remove mineral deposits from your kettle regularly.
• For an environmentally safe and inexpensive alternative to commercial cleaners, pour in a cup (250 mL) of vinegar and 3 cups (750 mL) water. Boil for a few minutes and rinse well.

Microwaves

- Many estimates say a microwave can use between 15% and 50% less energy than a conventional oven.
- Temperature probes will tell when food is done, and some automatically shut off the oven. If you have a probe, use it!
- The amount of energy saved depends on your cooking habits and the types of food you cook.
- Follow the manufacturer's instructions to prevent overcooking.
- Avoid using your microwave to defrost food—and remember that defrosting in the fridge saves energy by helping to keep the fridge cool.
- Avoid buying excessively packaged and highly processed ready-made microwave foods. The energy used to package and process cancels out and possibly exceeds any energy you save by using the microwave.
- Remember that the more food in the microwave, the longer it takes to cook. It may be better to use your regular oven for some large dishes. Check your instruction book.

SETTLING FOR MICROWAVE CAUTION

After weighing the evidence, we recommend the use of microwaves on the basis of the energy they save. But it's probably a good idea to keep abreast of the news on microwaves as it develops. Consumer publications are usually a good source of information. Always follow the safety precautions listed in your instruction manual. These include:

✳ Unplug your microwave when it is not in use.

✳ Make sure no food crumbs or edges of paper are left along the door seals. Radiation can leak out the cracks.

✳ Never lean on or put weight on the door. Radiation leakage could occur if the door becomes misaligned.

✳ Never store things in your microwave—except perhaps a cup of water. If someone accidentally turns it on, it's better to have water inside than nothing.

✳ Be sure your microwave won't open while it's on.

✳ Make sure worn door seals are replaced by authorized repair people.

✳ Never put wood or any kind of metal in your microwave. Don't forget that aluminum foil is a metal; metal will spark and damage your oven.

✳ Don't put glass crystal, earthenware not approved for microwave use, or recycled paper in your microwave; all may contain some metal.

✳ Watch out for dishes with metal—usually gold or silver—trim; they might ruin your microwave.

✳ Wipe out your microwave after every use. This not only prevents heavy-duty cleaning later, but a clean microwave cooks more efficiently.

✳ Microwaves made before 1971 had less stringent standards for the emission of non-ionizing radiation, so be extremely cautious about buying any used microwave. Also, the seals could be worn or the door misaligned.

✳ Stay about a yard (a metre) away from your microwave when it's on if you want to be extra-careful about avoiding the non-ionizing radiation. People wearing pacemakers should keep a safe distance away from an operating microwave.

MICROWAVES

Safe Cooking in the Microwave

Safe cooking in the microwave requires different information and standards than conventional cooking. Your owner's manual will have a good deal of essential information on cooking. However, to prepare a variety of recipes you will also need a good microwave cookbook. Follow all instructions carefully! Here are some important points to keep in mind:

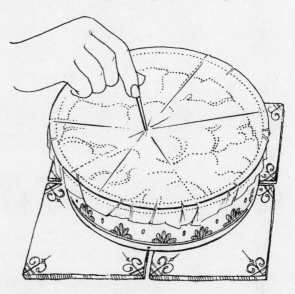

- Be careful about letting children use the microwave; it can be every bit as dangerous as a regular oven.
- Use potholders. Microwaves don't heat containers, but the food itself can; it can also splash out.
- Uncover cooked dishes away from your face; escaping steam can burn you.
- If you use plastic wrap as a cover, create an escape hole for steam by turning a bit of the edge back. Never puncture the wrap after cooking—steam can blast out and burn you.
- Foods with unpunctured skins, like whole tomatoes and eggs, can explode. Never cook whole eggs, and poke a few holes in foods like tomatoes and unpeeled potatoes before cooking.
- Puncture airtight coverings before cooking so steam can escape.
- Low-moisture foods like popcorn can combust, especially when cooked in a paper bag. If you make popcorn, a special microwave popcorn container is a far better choice than buying the microwavable popcorn in bags.

- Deep-frying in a microwave is dangerous.
- Never warm a baby bottle in the microwave; it can develop scalding hot spots. And throwaway plastic liners can explode.
- Never use the microwave for canning or sterilizing. The uneven heat can miss killing some of the potentially deadly bacteria.
- Some authorities say you should not use a microwave as the primary cooking source when preparing chicken and pork. The microwave's uneven cooking can leave little pockets of undercooked meat that can cause food poisoning or other illnesses.

• Microbes can also survive in other foods. To make sure food is safe:
  – Follow microwave cooking times and allow for standing time to help ensure that all bacteria are killed.
  – Stir and rotate foods as instructions require to make sure foods are cooked evenly, or you may get uncooked bits of food that are not safe to eat. Many foods and all liquids, like beverages, soups, and sauces, require stirring.
  – Cover dishes and arrange food uniformly. Add a little liquid to create steam that will help kill bacteria.
  – Place thicker portions toward the outer edges of the dish or plate.
  – Bacteria can survive on the food's surface, which stays cooler than the interior during microwaving. Prevent this by following instructions and allowing for standing time.
  – Meat cooks more thoroughly if it's been cut off the bones.
  – If you do use your microwave for primary cooking of chicken, note that a whole stuffed chicken definitely will not cook evenly; cook stuffing separately.
  – Probe meat with a meat thermometer in several places. Beef should be 160° F (70° C); veal, pork, and lamb at least 175° F (80° C), and poultry at least 185° F (85° C).
  – When reheating foods, cover them and be sure you get them piping hot—at least 160° F (70° C).

HOW MICROWAVES WORK

Microwave ovens contain a magnetron tube that radiates high-frequency radio waves into the inside of the oven. The energy from these beams passes right through substances like glass, wood, and plastic, but it is absorbed by fat, water, and sugar molecules. This absorbed energy causes the molecules to vibrate faster. This increased vibration creates friction, the friction creates heat—and the heat cooks the food.

Packaging, Plastics, Plastic Film Wraps, and the Microwave

There is concern over the use of plastics in the microwave. Some of the chemicals in certain additives used in the production of plastic may migrate—or leach—into the food. Although this may happen to some degree in the refrigerator, the probability increases greatly when the plastics are heated.

You may be surprised to learn that little is yet known about how plastics react to microwaving—even in the case of some of the plastics that microwave-ready foods are packaged in. There is, however, concern about some products. One is the heat-susceptor or "brown and crisp" packaging that is often used for products like microwave-ready fish sticks, french fries, popcorn, pizza, and waffles. Heat-susceptor packaging contains a plastic called polyethylene terephtalate or PET. The FDA approved the use of PET in the United States in containers like plastic pop bottles some years ago, but that was before they knew it would be used in microwaves. The FDA tested the product with heat in 1988 and found that leaching of plastics and other chemicals did occur. As a result, further testing is being carried out, and the FDA is still allowing its use in heat susceptors. Health and Welfare Canada also states that they have not seen any evidence to cause them great concern.

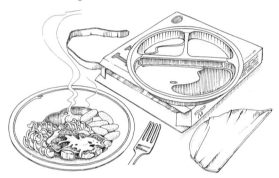

Excess packaging creates excess waste.

There is also concern about plastic film wraps when used in the microwave. Some brands may contain plasticizers that have been shown to leach into foods, particularly fatty foods, and especially at high temperatures.

PLASTIC AND FOOD SAFETY

Authorities disagree on whether any harm can come from the additives used in the production of plastic migrating into our food. Until more is known, it seems reasonable to use them cautiously for microwave cooking or food storage.

* Consider using reusable glass containers for storing foods in the refrigerator. However, not all glass containers can be frozen, so properly designed plastic containers are an alternative.

* If you choose to use plastic containers for food storage, your first choice should be those specifically designed for this purpose.

* If you choose to use old margarine tubs and the like, you may want to avoid storing fatty foods in them until more information is available. Dairy containers, such as yogurt containers, are probably acceptable for cold storage. But neither type of container should be used in the microwave.

* If you insist on using plastic film wrap—even though reusable containers with lids keep foods just as fresh—avoid letting it come in direct contact with the food.

* Don't let food come in contact with plastic that contains dyes, inks, or glues. For instance, it might not be a good idea to store vegetables from the garden for a long time in an inside-out plastic grocery or bread bag. The ink or dye on the printing may not be approved for food storage.

It is not known whether using materials containing these plasticizers in the microwave causes health problems, but it seems like a good idea to exercise caution. Until definitive studies are done, you might want to:

• Avoid heat-susceptor or "brown and crisp" packages. Even if they're proven safe, they are part of the excessive packaging problem.

• Avoid using microwave-ready foods wrapped in plastic. They too are excessively packaged, even if safe.

• Avoid using plastic film wrap—it's a throwaway product. But if you do use it in the microwave, keep the plastic from touching food, especially fatty food. Use it to cover a bowl, but not to wrap around food. Check for the microwave-safe symbol on the box. Even though it's not a regulated symbol, it should indicate that no questionable plasticizers are contained in the product.

The Society of the Plastics Industry of Canada recommends you don't microwave any plastic container for more than 10 minutes unless it's specifically designed for microwave use.

• It's probably best to avoid them altogether. A yogurt tub is safe for yogurt, but it probably hasn't been tested in the microwave.

• Avoid using plastic containers that become soft when heated.

• Avoid using any plastic—or paper—containing glues, dyes, or ink.

• Although the plastics industry says polystyrene is safe for normal microwave use, it does melt easily, and they admit that when it melts it gives off "noxious extractables." Styrene is a known carcinogen.

• It may be wise to use only plastics designed specifically for microwave use until more is known. And always follow manufacturer's instructions exactly.

• Consider using ceramics or glass instead of plastics.

MICROWAVE COOKWARE

Even though specially designed microwave cookware may be preferable to using old yogurt tubs in the microwave, the truth is that there is no way to be certain that your microwave plastics are safe. According to Health and Welfare Canada, no regulations are in place or under consideration for the label "microwave safe" on plastic containers or plastic wrap.

Food can be safely microwaved in oven-safe glass, like Pyrex, and glass-ceramic, like Corning Ware. Using these materials may be the best choice in the long run: you probably already have them on hand so you won't have to buy new; you can use them in your conventional oven, and they're generally trusted as they have been around for a long time. If you feel you absolutely need a set of special cookware, check out the article "Microwave Cookware" in *Canadian Consumer* magazine (No. 2, 1989) for recommendations on the best brands. Here are a few pointers to keep in mind:

✳ The shape of a dish affects how food cooks in it in the microwave. Food can be burnt on the edges and cold in the middle if done in a pan with square corners.

✳ Lids are important. Foods tend to cook faster and more evenly when heat can't escape.

✳ Dishes that keep the food warm are necessary so that heat is retained during "standing time."

✳ Wide, shallow dishes seem to lose heat faster than those that are narrower and deeper.

✳ Cookware that can go in the oven and in the microwave may be convenient, but check the labels carefully. Some can be heated only to average oven temperatures.

✳ Note that microwave "reheatable" cookware is designed only for reheating in the microwave; actual microwave cooking can't be done in it.

Slow cookers
- These can use up to 80% less energy than cooking the same thing on the range.
- They tend to work most efficiently when they're three-quarters full. If that's more than you need, freeze some for another meal.
- A slow cooker can save you money by making delicious meals out of the less-tender and less-expensive cuts of meat.
- Slow cookers are good for making dishes in which meat is a supplement rather than the main part of the meal.

Refrigerators and Freezers

Refrigerators use more energy than anything in the home except for water heaters and furnaces. Yet they're beneficial when we use them to store food so we don't have to go shopping so often, to keep food fresh so it doesn't spoil, and to store leftovers so they're not wasted.

Freezers also have their purpose—especially for families who grow their own vegetables or who buy and use large amounts of locally grown, in-season produce. If your freezer is used just to store overflow from your refrigerator's freezer compartment, you are wasting energy, money, and space. Plant a garden in the spring or start buying and freezing produce as it comes into season. Cook double the amount every time you use your conventional oven and freeze the extra. If you thaw it in the fridge and heat it up in the microwave, you'll be using your freezer to save energy, time, and money. Some cookware, like most ceramic glass, can be used in the freezer, oven, and microwave; it makes the whole process very easy.

Tips for Reducing Refrigerator Energy Costs

★ Don't place your fridge in a "hot" spot—near a radiator or in direct sun.

★ Set the dials no cooler than 37° F (3° C) for the fridge and 0° F (–18° C) for the freezer unit.

★ Turn off your butter warmer. It's actually a little heater and it makes your fridge work harder.

★ Test the seals by closing the door on a piece of paper. If the paper slips out easily when you pull it, you need new seals.

★ Defrost foods in the fridge. It helps cool the fridge.

★ Defrost manual-defrost freezer compartments as soon as you have 1/4 in (7 mm) of frost.

★ Decide what you want *before* you open the door. Standing with the door open wastes tremendous amounts of energy.

★ A full freezer compartment uses much less energy than an empty one. If your freezer is usually empty, place a few water-filled plastic containers in it and leave them there.

★ Cover all refrigerated foods, especially liquids. Moisture drawn into the air from uncovered foods makes your fridge work harder to keep things cool.

★ Vacuum the coils at the back of your fridge as soon as there is a noticeable accumulation of dust—usually two to six times a year. Be sure to unplug the fridge first.

★ Use adjustable shelves to maximize space and allow room for air circulation. Fridges don't cool efficiently if the air can't circulate.

★ For the same reason, never cram your fridge too full. Check your instruction manual for recommendations.

TIPS FOR ECONOMY FREEZING

★ The recommended temperature setting for freezers is 0° F (–18° C). No bacteria can grow at this temperature. Food stored at 10° F (–12° C) can be kept only half as long.

★ A freezer thermometer is a good investment.

★ Freezers operate at best efficiency when they are about two-thirds full.

★ When freezing several items at once, spread the packages out until they're frozen. Then stack them close together.

★ Freeze only as much food as your freezer can handle at one time—usually about 10 lb (5 kg) per 3.5 cu ft (100 L) of capacity. Otherwise you'll lower the temperature too much and your freezer will have to work overtime to raise it again.

★ Keep your freezer well organized so you don't spoil food by leaving it in too long or waste energy while you rummage around with the lid up.

★ Get a food-safe marker and label foods in large letters so you can find what you want quickly.

Food Plans

Once you have a freezer you might be tempted by the ads for food plans. These plans deliver to your home the food you need—except for perishables—for a certain period, for instance six months. The representatives for these plans say you'll save money because you won't be going to the store where you are tempted by expensive, unnecessary treats; you'll be able to budget better, and you'll avoid being surprised by price increases. It sounds reasonable, and many people are signing the contracts—often for as much as $2,000.

But caution is called for. The Office de la protection du consummateur du Québec found that once membership fees, delivery charges, and so on were considered, these plans didn't save the buyer much money. In fact, some people ended up paying 30% more for the food than they would have at the local market. And you still have to go to the store anyway to buy things like bread and fresh vegetables.

PROTEIN FROM PLANTS

Chapter Two may have made you decide it's time your family began eating lower on the food chain. Many environmentalists are calling for North Americans to eat at least one meatless meal a week. According to John Robbins's *Diet for a New America*, if North Americans ate just 10% less meat per year, the grain saved could feed 60 million people. The key here is *could*. If you eat less meat today, it doesn't mean that the resulting grain will automatically feed a hungry person. But it does mean that you are beginning to break away from the lots-of-meat-for-every-meal habit—a habit that is one of the reasons North Americans consume such a disproportionate amount of the world's resources.

If you are planning to eat one, or even several, meatless meals a week and continue to consume meat and dairy products, you don't have to calculate whether you're getting enough protein. Some estimates say most North Americans eat at least twice as much protein as they need.

You may want, however, to make eating low on the food chain the rule rather than the exception and only be hesitating because you think meatless meals are tasteless, boring, hard to prepare, and lacking in protein. Relax! None of these things are true. Try a few of the recipes scattered throughout this book, and you'll discover that meatless meals are delicious, exciting, fun to eat, and easy to prepare.

Adventuring Down the Food Chain

Even if you want to start eating lower on the food chain immediately, don't try to change your family's eating habits overnight.

* Begin by replacing meat-and-potatoes meals with main dishes that use meat or poultry as a supplement: soups, stews, goulashes, gumbos, casseroles, stir-frys, and pasta dishes.

* Gradually cut back on the meat in these recipes. Your family may not even notice.

* Dig out recipes for those old family favorites like macaroni and cheese. You may have a stack of meatless meals in your repertoire without realizing it.

* At first, cook at least one meatless meal a week, choosing ones that are fun and familiar instead of exotic and totally unfamiliar. Make a vegetarian pizza, bean tacos, or macaroni and cheese.

* If your family enjoys these dishes, move on to more experimental ones and those that don't even contain dairy products.

FUN FOODS FOR KIDS

Don't despair if you think your kids will never adjust to low-on-the-food-chain eating. None of kids' favorite snacks contain meat—and some low-meat and meatless dishes are already among their favorites:

* Spaghetti
* Macaroni and cheese
* Grilled cheese sandwiches
* Peanut butter and jelly
* Ravioli
* Pizza
* Chinese food

GREENING YOUR KITCHEN WITH INDOOR PLANTS

The color green has not come to symbolize the environmental movement by accident: few things are more environment-friendly than green growing plants, and they are wonderful to have in the green kitchen for many reasons. They help create a warm and pleasant atmosphere; they absorb carbon dioxide and replace it with fresh, pure oxygen; and recent tests have shown that several plants—including spider plants, potted mums, aloe vera, golden pothos, English ivy, and heart-leaf and lacy tree philodendrons—help remove certain pollutants from the air. Future testing may well show that even more plants do similar good work. Further, growing your own herbs is an excellent way to decorate and economize, and children love to get involved in indoor gardening projects.

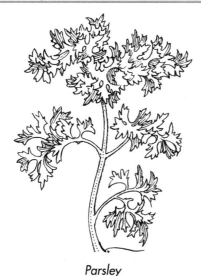

Parsley

GREENERY YOU CAN EAT!

Growing herbs indoors is simple—and if you've noticed how expensive fresh herbs are in stores, you know it is well worth your while. Most herbs that are easily grown outside can also be grown indoors. If you have a herb garden and want to enjoy them during the winter months, just pot a few in individual containers in the fall and bring them indoors. Be sure to wash off any spider mites or aphids with a mild solution of yellow naphtha soap and water before you bring them in.

Herbs can also be grown from seeds indoors. Simply follow the instructions on the seed package. If you create the right conditions, you should have success with chives, basil, tarragon, and chervil. Marjoram, thyme, dill, sage, savory, and rosemary can also do well indoors. Here are some pointers:

✳ Herbs will not do well if they have to endure great temperature fluctuations or too much heat and dry air. They must be placed well away from stoves or other heat-producing appliances.

✳ Herbs need from 30% to 50% humidity. If your kitchen is too dry, keep a bowl of water near them and use a mister.

✳ Herbs need good ventilation; they don't do well in stuffy air or in areas where greasy air can clog their pores.

✳ Most herbs need about five hours of direct sunlight a day. A few, such as chervil, the mints, and lemon balm, will grow in good, if not direct, light. If plants don't get enough

Gourmet Oils and Vinegars

These tasty but high-priced treats are easy to make at home when you have fresh herbs. Gourmet cookbooks abound with recipes. Here's one for Basil Oil from Mary McGrath, food writer at *The Toronto Star*:

2 cups	olive oil	500 mL
2	branches fresh basil, preferably with blossoms	2
1 1/2 tsp	black peppercorns	7 mL
1 1/2 tsp	coarse salt	7 mL
1	large strip sweet or hot red pepper	1

Place olive oil in a large bottle. Rinse basil; pat completely dry. Add basil, peppercorns, salt, and red pepper to oil. Cover tightly and store 1 week in cool, dark place.

Strain oil. Discard basil, peppercorns, salt, and red pepper. Store oil in tightly covered glass container in refrigerator. Use in salad dressing, with chicken or fish, tomatoes, pasta, potatoes, or for marinating fresh cheeses. Makes 2 cups (500 mL).

Basil   Marjoram

light, they tend to become tall and spindly. Rotate the containers regularly so that all sides get light.

* Different herbs can be planted in individual pots or together in a tray or indoor windowbox. They *must* have good drainage. The bottom of the container must be well lined with pebbles and/or pieces of broken terra cotta pots.

* Soil for herbs needs to be lighter than garden soil so that it drains well and doesn't compact. Rock-hard, dry soil has killed many indoor herbs. Try one of these mixtures: two parts loam to one part peat moss and one part vermiculite or perlite; or one part loam to one part peat moss, coarse sand, or fine-ground bark.

* Check the soil each day. If it is dry just below the surface, water the plant. They like room-temperature water. Although some leaves will always turn yellow and die, too many yellow leaves mean you are either over- or underwatering. Experiment to find the right balance.

Make Your Own Herb Mixes!

Stop paying those outrageous prices for mixed seasonings and make your own. Even some of the most exotic-sounding are simple to do:

Bouquet Garni is a bunch or "bouquet" of fresh or dried herb sprigs tied together with kitchen string, placed in a soup or stew for mild flavoring, and removed before serving. The bouquet is often made from 1 bay leaf, 3 sprigs chervil, 3 sprigs parsley, and 2 sprigs thyme. Sometimes a bit of orange peel is added, or the bouquet is tied inside a few stalks of celery.

Fines Herbes can be made by finely chopping: one part tarragon to two parts each chervil, chives, and parsley. Crumble the mixture together. If you like a little stronger tarragon flavor, combine all the herbs in equal amounts.

Poultry Seasoning is a combination of herbs. One that is good on poultry that will be browned or fried consists of equal amounts of paprika, sage, thyme, and oregano. One that is good for roasting fowl or soups consists of one part sweet marjoram to two parts each of basil, thyme, summer savory, and celery greens. You can then make your own poultry baking mix by combining about 2 Tbsp (25 mL) of your poultry seasoning with about 1/2 cup (75 mL) of corn meal and/or flour. Put the mixture in a clean paper bag and shake the chicken pieces in it to cover.

Whenever a recipe calls for parts of produce that are not usually eaten, such as orange or lemon rinds or celery greens, you should use certified organically grown produce.

Pesto

4	cloves garlic, chopped	4
2 cups	basil leaves, loosely packed	500 mL
4 Tbsp	freshly grated Parmesan cheese	50 mL
2 Tbsp	freshly grated Pecorino Romano cheese	25 mL
1/3 cup	pine nuts *or* walnuts *or* almonds	75 mL
1/2 tsp	salt	2 mL
1/2 cup	olive oil	125 mL

1. Using a blender, combine garlic, basil, cheeses, nuts, and salt. Gradually add oil to this paste and mix to a smooth sauce.
2. Makes 1 cup (250 mL). Toss with hot pasta.

Recipe courtesy *The Toronto Star*

COOKING WITH FRESH HERBS

Using fresh herbs in recipes is somewhat different from using the more common dried ones. Fresh herbs have a truer and more full-bodied flavor. When substituting fresh for dried in recipes, use about three times more of a fresh herb than a dried one.

Tips for Cleaning Produce

The only way you can be sure of getting pesticide-free produce is to grow your own or buy organic. If you do buy conventionally grown produce, eat a wide variety and:

✳ Keep in mind that the thicker the peel, the more protected the fruit or vegetable inside.

✳ Compost the outer leaves of leafy vegetables and the tops of vegetables like celery and carrots.

✳ Scrub your vegetables with a brush. Invest in a brush designed for this purpose—they are inexpensive and they do the job.

✳ Use a little pure soap in the water. Rinse it off very thoroughly.

✳ Wash broad, leafy vegetables, like spinach, carefully. They have a lot of surface for pesticides to settle on and wrinkles for the pesticides to catch in.

✳ Peel produce that has been waxed or wash it in water with a little detergent.

Plant foods, especially legumes and grains, are excellent sources of protein. The protein our bodies use is made up of 22 amino acids, in varying combinations. Eight of these amino acids are often called "essential" because they have to be obtained from outside food sources—our bodies cannot synthesize them.

The myth abounds that plant foods contain protein that is inferior to meat because many plant foods are "incomplete"; that is, they do not contain all eight amino acids in the proportions needed for our bodies to synthesize protein. If even one of these amino acids is present in a lower proportion than needed, the usability of the other amino acids is decreased accordingly. However, incomplete does not equal inferior. It is quite easy to obtain the essential amino acids from plant foods. People who eat a strictly vegetarian diet—just plant foods—can be as healthy as, if not far healthier than, people who rely heavily on meat.

Complementing Proteins: The Great Debate

But how can you be sure you are getting *enough* protein—especially the eight essential amino acids? Although eating a big chunk of meat is a handy way of fulfilling your daily protein requirements, that protein can also be obtained if you eat foods that lack certain amino acids along with foods that contain those particular amino acids within three or four hours of each other. Many of the world's traditional (and healthful) dishes combine complementary proteins: Mexican beans and tortillas, Middle Eastern falafel and pita, East Indian chapattis and lentils, and Chinese tofu and rice.

Many pure vegetarians do not worry at all about complementing proteins—and many are confident that they get more than enough complete protein as long as they consume enough calories and eat a wide variety of healthful whole grains, nuts, seeds, and legumes. However, no definite formula exists for determining how much protein any individual needs; some people definitely need more than the daily recommended allowance,

Easy Protein Complementing
Most protein complementing falls within four easy groups:
1) Whole grains with legumes
2) Nuts and seeds with legumes
3) Potatoes with milk products
4) Whole grains with milk products

and some scientists believe the recommended daily allowance should be raised by one-third. If you want to stop eating meat but want to be sure you'll still get enough protein, many good books on the subject can be found. Complementing proteins is really very easy. And, even if you're not concerned about protein, complementary plant proteins make up some of the most delicious dishes in the world.

Quick Bean Cooking

With traditional cooking methods, pre-soaking legumes can cut the cooking time in half. Clean and rinse the beans, put them in a large bowl, and cover them in double their volume of water. Leave them for about eight hours—overnight is perfect.

If you have forgotten to pre-soak your legumes, you can cut almost as much off your cooking time by parboiling them. Prepare them for cooking and bring the pot to a boil. Turn off the heat and let them soak for about an hour. Then proceed with your regular cooking.

Keep in mind that the cooking time listed in any recipe for legumes is an estimate. The age of the beans, where they were grown, and the hardness of the cooking water can all affect the cooking time.

The Pressure Cooker

Grandma knew a good thing when she used a pressure cooker to whip up meals! The lowly pressure cooker, which has been virtually forgotten in this age of high-tech, cooks many foods three times faster than conventional methods. Depending on the food, a pressure cooker can save you as much cooking time and energy as a microwave—and in some cases it even cooks faster than a microwave. And you can buy a pressure cooker for a fraction of the cost of a microwave.

THEY'RE SAFE!

If you're about to skip to the next section because stories from your childhood have convinced you that a pressure cooker is nothing more than a time-bomb about to decorate your ceiling with garbanzo beans, read on. The days of the exploding pressure cooker are long gone. With modern technology, pressure cookers are virtually impossible to explode. In fact, only by wantonly flouting the manufacturer's instructions could you come close to blowing one up. *Protect Yourself* magazine recently tested eight popular pressure cookers and couldn't make any of them blow up even when they intentionally blocked the regulators. Pressure cookers made today have a safety valve that releases steam if the internal pressure becomes too high, and for those cooks who aren't comforted by one safety valve there are now pressure cookers with two safety valves. These brands include the T-Fal Sensor and the Presto Express.

Another safety feature available on many modern pressure cookers is a safety lock on the lid that makes it impossible to open the pot while the contents are still under pressure. Even without the lock, you would have to be exceptionally strong to open a pressure cooker before it cools down. Of course, to ensure safe usage, you need to read and follow the manufacturer's instructions, just as you do with any appliance.

A Must for the Green Kitchen

Pressure cookers are especially handy for cooking those low-on-the-food-chain foods like legumes and grains that you'll be using in the green kitchen. Kidney beans, for example, can be pressure-cooked in 30 minutes, while they take around two hours to cook on the stove, even when they have been pre-soaked. (One of the greatest joys of the pressure cooker is that it allows you to make meals based on legumes without a lot of planning or pre-preparation.) Medium-sized potatoes can be done in the pressure cooker in 15 minutes instead of 45 in the oven.

Pressure cookers also give you a tremendous nutritional advantage: the short cooking time and the small amount of water needed retain nutrients and colors. These utensils keep foods at the peak of flavor by trapping in natural juices. In short, they are one of the best pieces of equipment you can possibly have in the green kitchen.

ENERGY-EFFICIENT COOKING

* Pressure cooking, steaming, and microwaving can all produce food of fairly comparable nutritive value—and all require less time than conventional methods. This can equal a big energy saving.

* These methods also require less water than conventional cooking. The less water used, the less energy required to heat it.

* Pressure cookers and steamers can be equipped with dividers so that you can cook two or three vegetables at once—on one burner.

* You can cook several vegetables at once in your microwave. This represents an energy saving as long as the extra quantity doesn't increase the cooking time too much.

* An added bonus: the less time you cook and the less water you use, the fewer vitamins are lost in cooking.

Curried Rice and Lentils

1	(28 oz/796 mL) can tomatoes	1
1	large onion	1
1 tsp	coriander	5 mL
1 tsp	cumin	5 mL
1 tsp	cayenne pepper	5 mL
1 tsp	garam masala	5 mL
1 cup	lentils	500 mL
1 cup	brown rice	500 mL
	Oil	

1. Drain the tomatoes, reserving the juice. Add water to the juice to make up 6 cups (1.5 L) liquid.
2. Chop onion in bite-sized chunks. Add to pressure cooker with oil (use a little more oil than you normally would for one onion) and fry until onion is clear.
3. Lower the heat and add the spices. (The amounts given are only suggestions. Note: *All* spices can be replaced with a commercial curry powder to taste.) Stir quickly. The mixture will become very dry.
4. Quickly add the tomatoes and the cooking liquid. Stir well. The spices tend to stick a little to the bottom, so be sure they are scraped up into the liquid or they will scorch.
5. Add the lentils and rice. Bring the pressure cooker to 15 lb (50 kPa) pressure. Cook for about 10 minutes.
6. Serve with chapattis and a yogurt and cucumber salad. Serves 2 to 3.

How Pressure Cookers Work

The boiling point of water increases or decreases with changes in the air pressure. At sea level, water boils at 212° F (100° C). A pressure cooker pressurizes the cooking water and raises its boiling point. At 15 lb (50 kPa) of pressure, for example, water boils at 232° F (111° C). The food inside cooks faster because of these higher temperatures. The shorter cooking times save energy—and destroy fewer nutrients than conventional cooking.

PRESSURE COOKER SAFETY

Always read and follow the manufacturer's instructions for operating your pressure cooker. It is a safe kitchen tool, but like most appliances, it can cause safety problems if misused. Follow the guidelines below, and check your instruction booklet for the specifics on each:

* Do not cook beans that froth, such as split peas.
* Most models should never be filled more than two-thirds full for solids, for instance a whole chicken, and one-half full for grains and legumes.
* Never try to open the lid when it's difficult to do so—it means the contents are still under pressure.
* Some models have a regulator that simply lifts off by hand. Never remove it while there is any pressure in the pot; the steam will shoot out and can burn you.

PRESSURE COOKING TIPS

* Cook several different foods, perhaps your whole meal, in the pressure cooker at once by using dividers.
* Eliminate sticking and get rid of the fuss of measuring the right amount of water for grains:
  - put about an inch (2.5 cm) of water in the pressure cooker
  - put your grain, rice for instance, into a stainless steel bowl
  - be sure there will be some space between the sides of the bowl and the pot and considerable space between the top of the bowl and the lid of the pot
  - pour in water until it is about 3/4 in (2 cm) above the rice
  - lower the bowl into the pressure cooker and pressure cook as usual.
* You can use this method to cook legumes and rice at the same time. Just put the proper amount of water, beans, and spices into the pot and set the stainless steel bowl with the rice and water in it down in the middle.
* To cook foods that require different times, begin with the food that requires the most cooking and add the others when appropriate. To cool your pressure cooker quickly so you can add the next ingredient, follow the manufacturer's instructions: for some brands you simply set the pressure cooker in the sink and run a small stream of cold water on the lid. Do not lift off the regulator—the steam can burn you.
* Pre-soaking isn't necessary for quick-cooking legumes like lentils, but it can drastically reduce the time for longer-cooking beans like garbanzos and kidney beans.
* You may sometimes want to decrease the amount of spices you would normally use, as there is less liquid to dilute their taste.
* Always use the specified amount of water—it's needed to make the steam.

THE WONDERFUL WOK

When you're looking for energy-efficient and nutritious ways to cook, don't forget the wok.

* A tasty stir-fry can be ready in just a few minutes.

* A wok with a lid can be used for steaming vegetables and making fluffy, moist Chinese rolls for dim sum.

* To cook ingredients that require different times—and to avoid wasting energy by overloading your wok—purchase one of the mesh holding screens that clamps onto the side of the wok. Cook each type of vegetable separately, and scoop it onto the screen when it's done. Dump all the vegetables back into the wok for a few minutes at the end so the flavors blend.

* If you don't have a holding screen, begin with the vegetables that require the most cooking, and then cook those that require less and less time in order. For example:
  - Large pieces of broccoli with stems
  - Zucchini—unless very thinly sliced
  - Onions
  - Green peppers
  - Mushrooms
  - Bean sprouts

Crunchy Stir-Fry

1	large onion	1
1	clove garlic, minced	1
1	large green pepper	1
1/2	head bok choy	1/2
1/2 lb	mushrooms	500 g
1/4 lb	bean sprouts	250 g
	Oil for cooking	
1 cup	cashews	250 mL
1/4 cup	sesame seeds	125 mL
	Soy sauce to taste	

1. Clean and chop the vegetables into bite-sized chunks. (The amounts and types of vegetables are flexible, but the ones above make a good flavor combination.)

2. In a wok over high heat, heat the oil. (Use an oil that can withstand the high heat of the wok. Peanut oil is a good choice.)

3. Add the vegetables in the order listed. As soon as one is about half-cooked, add the next. The vegetables should still be crunchy when done. The bean sprouts need only to be heated through, so add them when the mushrooms are almost exactly like you want them.

4. Stir in the nuts and seeds; add soy sauce. Cover the wok so the flavors steam together for about a minute.

5. Serve immediately over rice. Serves 2.

This recipe is also good with chicken breast and shows how poultry can be used as a supplement rather than the main part of the meal. Use one whole breast. Cut the meat off the bones, cut it into bite-sized chunks and marinate in a little garlic and soy sauce. Cook the chicken first; when no pink remains, add the vegetables as described. (Don't throw the bones away. Freeze them, and add them to the homemade chicken soup you make. The bones from three whole breasts are enough to make a light and delicious broth.)

PLAY IT AGAIN!

The Creative Use of Leftovers

It's time we took a lesson from the Europeans who, when faced with leftovers, are at their creative best. They take great pride in turning a few unappetizing odds and ends into anything from a succulent stew to a tantalizing curry. They consider the North American habit of throwing out leftovers a crime. We need to begin thinking the same way—for the sake of both the world and our wallets.

Using leftovers creatively takes only a little imagination. Chop up that leftover meat, toss it into the wok with a few fresh vegetables, and season with garlic and soy sauce for a delicious stir-fry. Make vegetable fried rice with leftover rice and a few chopped mushrooms and green peppers. Turn leftover cooked vegetables into a Russian salad or toss them into a soup. Purée last night's salad vegetables with some tomato juice and a few herbs to make an instant cup of gazpacho. Freeze leftover pancakes and waffles to create your own inexpensive, unpackaged version of toaster pop-ups.

There is no limit to the creative things you can do with leftovers. Here are a few ideas; for more, check your library — whole cookbooks are dedicated to the subject.

Broiled Fish and Rice Toss

Here is an unusual and exceptionally tasty way to use leftover fish. The amounts given are variable and depend only on how much fish you have and how many people you need to feed. The secret of this dish is to combine everything while it is hot. Time it so the vegetables are done when the rice is still piping hot.

Cooking oil
Onion, diced
Green and/or red peppers, diced
Mushrooms, sliced
Cooked rice
Leftover broiled fish, boned and diced

1. Cook rice, or reheat leftover rice in the microwave.
2. Fry the onions in a little oil. Just as they start to become clear, add the peppers. When the peppers are partially cooked, add the mushrooms. Stir and cook for just a minute more. The peppers should be crunchy and the other vegetables must not be overcooked.
3. Toss together the rice, vegetables, and fish in a large serving bowl.
4. Serve immediately either as a one-dish meal or with a salad.

Boney Maroney Soup

Few sights are sorrier than a platter covered with the remains of a roast chicken or turkey. But given a little time those bones can be turned into a delicate, flavorful soup stock. Once the stock is made you can toss in just about anything you find in the fridge, from leftover chicken to cooked vegetables.

Stocks made from cooked chicken or turkey bones are much lighter and more delicate in flavor than those made from raw poultry. Because of this, some cooks like to throw a chicken bouillon cube into the pot. This, of course, won't do for purists!

There are no hard and fast rules for making this soup. You must only be sure you have enough bones. The remains of the Thanksgiving turkey provide more than enough, and those of a large chicken are usually adequate, but many cooks like to freeze and save the bones of two or three chickens before they begin. Here are the basic steps:

1. Place the bones of one cooked turkey or two medium chickens in a soup pot. If you disjoint and/or chop the bones to some degree, the stock will be more flavorful. Add the drippings from the cooking pan. Cover with cold water.
2. Add two peeled cloves garlic and a whole peeled onion (stick a few cloves in it if you like). For seasoning, add a bouquet garni or a bay leaf and thyme. If you have a wilty carrot or a few celery tops, clean thoroughly and add them too.
3. Bring to a boil, lower the heat, and simmer very gently for a minimum of 2 hours. Traditionally, stocks are cooked uncovered, but propping the cover open so there's a good-sized crack works, too.
4. Strain the broth to remove bones and vegetable pieces; gently squeeze the juice out of the onion. Wash the pot, return the stock to the pot, and bring back to a simmer.
5. Wash and dice a selection of fresh vegetables such as celery, onions, potatoes, beans, leeks, mushrooms, and carrots. Add to the simmering stock and cook for about 15 minutes or until the vegetables are done. Leftover cooked vegetables can be added at any time or puréed first and added to thicken and flavor the stock. If you have leftover macaroni or shell pasta, add it a minute before serving.

Mashed Potato Cakes

Throwing out leftover potatoes is a shame — not only because of the waste but also because so many delicious things can be made with them. Baked potatoes can be sliced, dabbed with butter, and broiled in the toaster oven. Baked and boiled potatoes can be cubed and used in a frittata or to make home-fries. Mashed potatoes can be put in muffin cups and browned under the broiler for an attractive side dish or used as the topping for shepherd's pie. Here's another creative use for mashed potatoes:

Mashed Potato and Herb Balls

2 cups	leftover mashed potatoes	500 mL
2	eggs, separated	2
1 Tbsp	each chopped fresh parsley and/or chives or other fresh herbs	15 mL

1. Reheat mashed potatoes in the microwave or with a little milk in a thick-bottomed saucepan.
2. Mix in fresh herbs. (You may substitute 1/4 tsp (1 mL) or less dried herbs for each tablespoon of fresh herbs.) You might even add a little crushed fresh garlic if you like. Beat in the egg yolks. Let the mixture cool a little.
3. Beat egg whites until stiff; gently fold into potato mixture.
4. Form into balls, place on a greased cookie sheet, and bake at 350° F (180° C), turning occasionally, until crisp.

CHAPTER FOUR
STORING AND PRESERVING FOODS

Creating a green kitchen has as much to do with our attitude as it does with the kinds of pots, pans, appliances, and foods we use. At the foundation of this attitude is an understanding of the *true* cost of food. Here in North America our food is so inexpensive that most of us don't realize its true value.

Consider, for a moment, a loaf of bread. Since it costs only a dollar or so, we tend to think of it as very cheap. Many of us think nothing of using half a loaf and, if the rest goes stale after a day or two, throwing it out. We never stop to consider the labor and fossil fuels that went into growing and threshing the fields of wheat, the vast amounts of power it took to transport the grain and mill it, the effort and energy it took to prepare the dough and bake it, or the energy and natural resources that were used in packaging and transportation.

When we *do* consider all this, our attitude changes. We begin to see how costly—and valuable—a 99-cent loaf of bread really is. The same is true of everything we eat.

This doesn't mean we need to become fanatical about food. But it does mean we need to develop a healthy respect for it, learn to store it so it lasts as long as possible, and avoid wasting it.

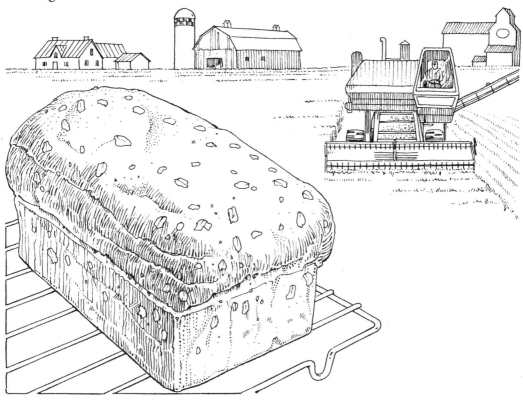

HOW TO STORE FOODS TO AVOID WASTE

Earlier generations had a greater regard for food than many of us have today. It cost them proportionately more, and it was generally harder to come by. Many of the ways they cared for and stored food are as useful now as they were then. Modern home economics and food sciences have also added to our understanding of how to make food last. Amazingly simple things can make a big difference in how well our food keeps. Mushrooms, for example, will last two to three times longer in a paper bag than they will in a plastic one. This section offers more ideas on how to store food and avoid waste.

Fruits and Vegetables

The fresher fruits and vegetables are when you buy them, the longer they'll keep. Remember that produce may appear fresh when it really isn't. It may have been waxed, irradiated, or kept for long periods in cold storage. Regardless of the means used to make a plant appear fresh, enzymes begin to cause oxidation and the loss of vitamins A, B, and C as soon as the plant is harvested. Buying locally grown, in-season produce is one way to help ensure you're getting the freshest fruit and vegetables possible. Of course, the only way you can be guaranteed absolute freshness is to grow your own or visit pick-your-own farms.

While you do want to buy produce that is fresh, you don't want to be too concerned about irregularities in size and shape or small marks on fruits and vegetables. If we want farmers to use fewer pesticides and fertilizers, we have to learn to accept imperfections in our produce.

Apples
- Buy firm apples that do not yield when gently pressed.
- Wrap freshly picked apples individually in newspaper and store them in a cool, dry place, like a root cellar; they'll keep for months.

Artichokes
- Buy plump, heavy artichokes with tightly clinging leaves.
- Wrap them, unwashed, in a damp cotton cloth and place in a reusable plastic bag in the fridge; they'll stay fresh for about a week.

Asparagus
- Look for closed, compact tips and mostly green stalks.
- Trim a little off each stalk, cut an X in the bottom, store upright in the fridge in a container with an inch of water.

Avocados
- Avoid cutting into an unripe avocado by sticking a toothpick in the stem end. If it slides in and out with ease, the avocado is ripe.
- Store at room temperature until ripe, then store in the fridge and use as soon as possible.

Bananas
- Bananas are best for eating when they are solid yellow with a few brown flecks.
- Store in the fridge if you need to keep them a while. Most people do not do this because the skin turns black, but the fruit keeps longer.

Beets
- Choose firm, smooth, dark-red beets. Wilted tops usually mean they are not fresh, but if the flesh is firm they can be okay.
- Remove tops before storing in the fridge—and remember, the nutrient-rich tops are delicious when steamed.

Berries
- Check the bottom of the berry container and buy only those that are dry. A damp or stained container may mean some of the fruit is overripe or moldy.
- Choose blueberries that are dark blue with a silvery cast.
- Store berries loosely packed in a covered container; refrigerate immediately.
- Freeze blueberries without washing and they'll keep their color and shape. Wash frozen berries just before using.
- Refrigerate raspberries or blackberries and use as soon as possible; avoid those with attached stem caps.
- Choose firm, bright red strawberries with their stems attached. Remove stems as soon as berries are washed; the stems soak up water and make the berries mushy. Store strawberries in a colander in the fridge. This allows air to circulate around them and keeps them fresher longer.

Broccoli
- Look for firm, tight clusters of buds, and avoid yellow or wilted leaves and overly thick stems.
- Store in the fridge; use within 3 to 5 days.

Cantaloupe
- Choose cantaloupes with no stems and ones that give slightly when pressed on the stem end and smell flavorful.
- Ripen at room temperature, refrigerate, and use fairly soon.

Cherries
- Choose firm but not hard fruit. Avoid those with dried stems or leaking flesh.
- Ripen at room temperature, refrigerate, and use immediately.

To speed up ripening of immature peaches, pears, avocados, tomatoes, bananas, or melons, place them under a glass dome— or in a tightly closed plastic bag. This traps the escaping ethylene gas and speeds ripening. Throw in an apple, which gives off a great deal of ethylene, and the fruit will ripen even faster. Don't try this with cherries, berries, grapes, or oranges— you'll end up with mush.

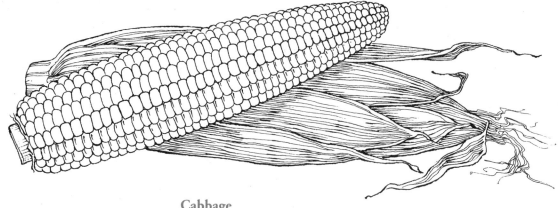

Cabbage
- Choose cabbages that feel heavy for their size.
- Although they'll keep for quite a while in the fridge, they are best used within 2 weeks.

Carrots
- Avoid carrots with large green areas at the top.
- Cut carrot greens off before storing; they can suck moisture out of the carrots.
- Store in the fridge or in mesh bins in a cool, dry place.

Cauliflower
- Look for tight buds and a creamy-white color; avoid those with discoloration.
- Store in the fridge; best within 2 weeks.

Corn
- Look for soft, moist silk; avoid cobs with dried or discolored stems.
- Store in the fridge with husks on; the sooner eaten, the sweeter.

Cucumbers
- Check for soft, shriveled, or wilted ends before you buy.
- White or pale-green areas are fine; very bumpy skin often indicates a tasty cucumber.
- Store unwrapped in the fridge; use within a week.

Eggplants
- Look for heavy, firm eggplants with uniform dark purple skin.
- Store eggplants at room temperature—around 60° F (15° C) is perfect.

Lemons
- Choose fruit that is heavy for its size and has fairly thin, smooth skin.
- Keep at room temperature or in the fridge for up to 2 weeks.

Lettuce

- Iceberg lettuce should give slightly when squeezed. Romaine should have loosely folded leaves.
- Core iceberg lettuce and wash by running water into the hole.
- Both types keep far better and rust more slowly if washed, dried well, and stored in a moisture-free container. Special plastic-ware containers with racks to keep the lettuce off the bottom are a good investment.
- Limp lettuce—or celery—can be crisped by placing it in a pan of cold water with a few slices of raw potato.

Mushrooms

- Choose mushrooms that have closed or just slightly open caps; the gills should be pink or light tan, not brown.
- Store in a paper bag. When ready to use, clean by wiping with a damp towel and trimming just a little off the stem. Small bad spots can also be trimmed away.

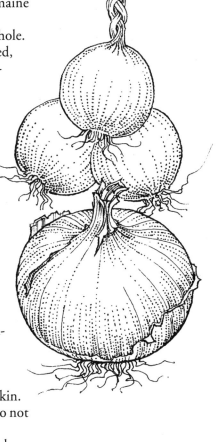

Onions

- Store in a cool, dark place.
- They keep longer hanging in a cotton-mesh bag or a grid-style stacking bin than in a closed bag.

Oranges

- Choose fruit that is heavy for its size with fairly smooth skin.
- Greenish areas at the stem end or slight brown spotting do not affect quality.
- Store at room temperature or in the fridge for up to 2 weeks.

Peaches

- Look for creamy or yellowish fruit with red patches; they should be firm or just a little soft.
- Ripen at room temperature, refrigerate, and eat in 3 to 5 days.

Pears

- Bartletts should be pale to deep yellow; Anjou should be light to yellowish green; Bosc should be greenish or brownish yellow.
- Avoid skin that is dull or breaking down near the stem.
- Store at room temperature in a paper bag until the stem end gives slightly when pressed.
- Refrigerate and use in 5 days or less.

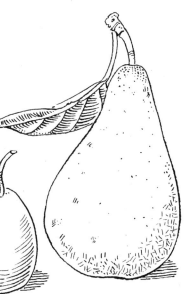

Plums

- Choose firm to slightly soft fruit.
- Store at room temperature until the fruit yields to pressure. Then refrigerate and use within 3 to 5 days.

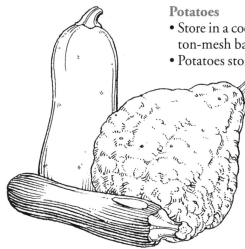

Potatoes
- Store in a cool, dark place. They'll keep longer hanging in a cotton-mesh bag or a grid-style stacking bin.
- Potatoes stored in the fridge will become sweet and mushy.

Rhubarb
- Look for stems that have lots of pink or red and are not too slender or too thick.
- Store in fridge and use within 3 to 5 days.

Squash
- Look for firm summer squash (zucchini); avoid ones with dull skin.
- Look for winter squash that is heavy for its size with a tough, hard rind.
- Store both at room temperature—60° F (15° C). Use summer squash within a week. Winter squash stored in a cool, dark, dry place will keep for months.

String Beans
- Snap one in half before you buy. If it breaks easily, it's fresh.
- Store in the fridge and use within a week.

Tomatoes
- Ripen green tomatoes at room temperature, but away from sunlight.

Watermelon
- Flick your index finger against the melon. A nice, high *plink* means it's ripe. A *thunk* means it isn't.
- Look for firm, smooth, dullish melons with yellowish or creamy white—not green or stark white—undersides.
- Wrap in newspaper or damp burlap before you take it on a picnic and it will stay cool.
- Store at cool room temperature or refrigerate.

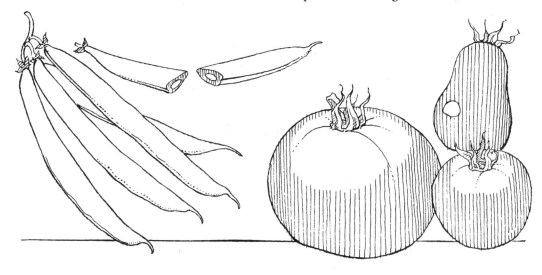

SMART SHOPPING

One of the best ways to prevent waste is to avoid buying too much and being influenced by grocery store marketing techniques. Here are some tips that will help you buy only what you need—and save you money in other ways too.

✳ Plan weekly menus and shop with a list.

✳ Go down each aisle only once. When you go back to an aisle a second time you tend to be tempted by unnecessary items.

✳ Resist impulse buying! Studies show that we are particularly susceptible to high-priced, unplanned purchases when we begin shopping and our cart has only a few items in it!

✳ Shop in less than half an hour. One study shows that the amount we spend per minute goes way up after the first 30 minutes in the store.

✳ Shop alone if you've ever noticed that you make far more unplanned purchases when you have "help."

✳ Watch out for store manipulation techniques and don't be tricked: higher-priced items are often at eye-level, while you have to bend down to get staples; items may be placed in special displays at the ends of the aisles to make you *think* they are on sale; individually wrapped candy—much more expensive than the bulk—is placed near the checkout lines where it will catch your children's eye.

✳ Be sure coupons represent good deals—and use them only to buy things you *really* need.

✳ Never shop on an empty stomach. Studies show you're much more susceptible to impulse buying when you're hungry.

Dairy Products

All fresh dairy products need to be refrigerated if they are going to be stored for more than a day. Products like canned and UHT (ultra-heat treated) milk, of course, will keep unopened in the cupboard for months. Always buy the freshest dairy products you can. Best-before labels have taken the guesswork out of buying dairy products. Be sure to check them—they are there to help you avoid waste!

Milk, cream, butter, and other dairy products should be well covered or wrapped for storage so they do not absorb odors from the fridge.

• Refrigerated eggs keep for a fairly long time, but most authorities recommend using them within 2 weeks.

• Grade AAA eggs are the freshest; AA are somewhat less fresh, and so on. B eggs are generally sold only to restaurants and institutions.

• Unsure about the freshness of an egg? Put it in a glass of water. If it lies flat it's fresh; if it stands upright it's older; if it floats it's stale.

• Cheese should be kept in tightly sealed containers. A few sugar cubes are said to keep mold from forming.

• Soften hardened cheese by soaking it in buttermilk. And to stop cheese you're not going to use for a while from getting hard in the first place, rub butter on it.

• Rescue frozen cream cheese or ricotta that has turned grainy by whipping it smooth again.

• Turn your cottage cheese container upside down and the cheese will keep better.

Legumes and Dried Vegetables

Legumes are the vegetables, like beans and peas, that grow in pods on long, running stems. Generally dried for storage, they come in a variety of shapes and colors including everything from tiny red lentils to large white lima beans. People have been cultivating legumes for millennia, but most of those we use today came into use in the past two thousand years.

Legumes contain vitamins, minerals, and fiber and are an excellent source of protein and complex carbohydrates. They are extremely filling—and not nearly as high in calories as is popularly believed.

- Buy legumes in stores with a rapid turn-over. Look for ones that have a rich color and are plump. Uniform size ensures even cooking time. Pale, wrinkled beans are getting on.
- Store legumes in tightly closed glass jars in a cool, dry place.
- They keep well for six months to a year. After that they take longer to cook and often become grainy.
- Legumes stored on an open shelf look attractive and remind you to use them more often.
- Before using, pick out shriveled, broken, or discolored beans. Then wash. Any old ones you've missed will float to the surface.

> Dried foods must be kept moisture-free to preserve freshness. Keep them all in tightly closed containers—glass is preferable. The cupboard they are stored in should be clean, cool, ventilated, and well away from the heat and steam of the stove and refrigerator exhausts. Since sunlight as well as heat can cause dried foods to break down, be sure the bulk-storage jars you keep on open shelves are in shaded parts of the kitchen.

Grains and Flours

Grains are the cereal grasses like wheat, rye, millet, oats, and rice. The cultivation of grains marked the beginning of agriculture for those ancient tribes that once had to forage for food.

Whole grains, those that retain the germ and bran, are far more nutritious than processed grains; however, they have a much shorter shelf-life so they need to be stored with care and used before they become rancid. A good sniff will usually tell you if grain is still good—rancid grain has a sharp, sour smell.

- Choose a bulk food store that has a rapid turn-over so that you get fresh grain.
- Look for plump, unshriveled individual grains that are uniform in size and color.
- Store in tightly closed glass jars in a cool, dry place.
- Properly stored grains keep for several months, but the sooner they're used the better. Rotate your supply so you use the oldest grains first.
- Grains sometimes harbor mealworm eggs. These harmless but unpleasant creatures hatch in warmth and humidity. They are almost impossible to see. Brown rice is par-

ticularly susceptible, so you might like to rinse it in a fine sieve before cooking.
• Keeping a few bay leaves in the jar is said to "prevent" meal-worms.

Flours and Meals

Grains are milled to produce flours and meals; meals are more coarsely ground than flours. Milling releases the natural oils, so flours and meals don't last as long as the unmilled grains. Highly processed flours no longer contain the bran and germ. Whole-grain flours do and, consequently, have to be stored far more carefully; they do not have a long shelf-life unless refrigerated.
• Buy your whole flours and meals from a health food store that has a rapid turn-over so you can be sure of freshness.
• Store flours and meals in moisture-proof containers in a very cool, dry place. They absorb moisture easily and will go bad quickly once they do.
• Refrigerate whole-grain flours if you are going to keep them for more than two months. In the summer, it is probably best to refrigerate them right away.
• Buy the kinds of flours you use only occasionally in small quantities.
• In general, don't buy more flour than you'll use in two to three months.

Breads and Pasta

Flours are used most commonly in the making of breads and pastas, and these two nutritious foods form the staples of many diets around the world. All breads made without preservatives have a short shelf-life—but storage methods can make a real difference.

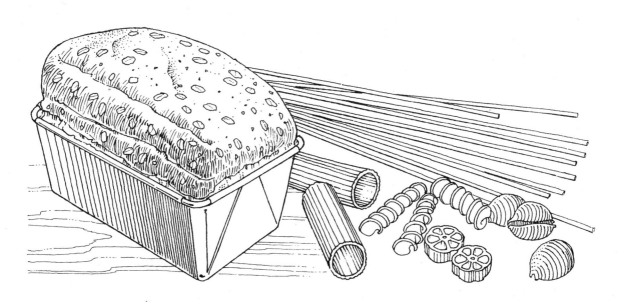

- The bread box has stood the test of time; keep it in a cool, dry corner of the kitchen.
- In many European countries fresh whole-grain bread is kept in a bag made of soft, unbleached cotton; stored inside a bread box, this keeps bread quite fresh.
- Breads made with yeast keep much better than "quick" breads, those made with baking soda or powder. Plan to use quick breads in one day—or toast them the next.
- Store pasta in tightly covered glass jars in a cool, dry place. It will keep for several months.
- Whole-grain pastas keep better in the fridge during the summer.

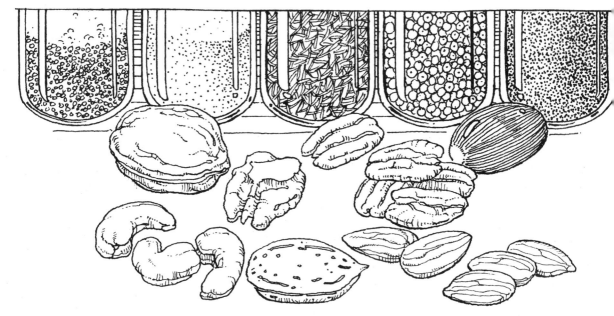

Nuts and Seeds

Nuts and seeds were once a staple for the nomadic tribes who foraged for food. Later, as civilization spread, nuts and seeds became highly prized delicacies. Nuts, a hard-shelled fruit, come from nut trees—except for the peanut, which is actually a legume. Edible seeds come from various fruits and flowering plants. Most nuts and seeds are extremely rich in protein, vitamins, and minerals, but they are also high in fat. This high fat content means nuts do not keep well. Once they are shelled, rancidity can set in quickly.

- Buy your nuts and seeds—especially shelled ones—from a store that has a rapid turn-over.
- Nuts in the shell can be kept in airtight containers in a cool, dry place for several months in the cool seasons. But they keep better in the fridge in the hot, humid summer.
- Shelled nuts and seeds, if very fresh when purchased, will keep one to two months in tightly closed glass jars. Keep them dark and cool. The fridge is best in the summer.

- Nuts are in season—and freshest—in the fall and winter.
- Refrigerate pine nuts. They spoil easily.
- Chestnuts should be used immediately or refrigerated. They are almost vegetable-like, as they are nearly 50% water.
- Pack shelled nuts and seeds in airtight containers and freeze. They keep for up to a year.
- Check nuts, particularly peanuts, for mold. Moldy nuts must be discarded, as they can be contaminated with a naturally occurring toxin, aflatoxin.

Cooking Ingredients

We sometimes don't give a great deal of thought to the storage of ingredients used in cooking, like dried fruit, sweeteners, seasonings, and oils, but they too can last longer and retain their flavour if they are stored properly.

- Store dried fruits in airtight containers in a dark, cool place; they can keep for up to a year.
- But eat them sooner rather than later. Over time they lose moisture and become tougher. Also, vitamin C deteriorates over time.
- If stored in too warm a place, dried fruits can ferment and be ruined.
- Honey will keep for an indefinite time in a covered container at room temperature. Usable honey has been retrieved from ancient Egyptian tombs!
- Crystallized honey is still fine; it can be liquefied by warming the jar slowly in a pan of water on very low heat or in the microwave for a few moments.
- Store brown sugar in a tightly closed jar with a slice of apple to keep it from getting hard.
- If brown sugar has hardened, add a piece of bread and it will soften. Then remove the bread.
- No one ever uses a whole gingerroot! Keep it from going bad by washing, peeling, and chopping it into 1/8 in (3 mm) slices. Put it in a clean glass jar and cover with sherry. The ginger will keep for months, and afterwards you can add the spicy sherry to a marinade.
- To save time, peel all the cloves from a head of garlic at once, cover them with oil, and store in a tightly closed jar. The flavored oil is then great for salads.
- Many other herbs and spices can be stored in distinctive and flavorful ways. Check the special section on herbs in Chapter Three.
- Refined oils will keep up to a year in a cool, dark, dry place.
- Unrefined or lightly refined oils will keep from four to six months. But they *must* be kept cool and dark. Refrigerate in summer.
- Oils rich in monosaturates (e.g., olive and peanut oil) may thicken and turn cloudy in the fridge, but they are still fine. To bring back to normal, measure out the amount you need and let it stand at room temperature awhile.

SAVING FOOD AND KEEPING IT SAFE

You undoubtedly know that it is important to keep food from spoiling in order to protect yourself and others, especially those with lower resistance such as children and the elderly, from possible illness. But keeping food safe is also an important aspect of running a green kitchen. Good use is made of leftovers and food is properly stored so it doesn't go bad and have to be thrown out.

A surprising number of simple food safety precautions are routinely ignored: Someone will not bother to wash off a can opener, not realizing that the little bits of food left on the blade can easily spoil at room temperature and infect the food in the next can that is opened; a cook will set a hot pan or lid on a wooden chopping block, not knowing that the increased warmth can cause the bacteria trapped in the crevices to flourish; or a backyard chef will place the nicely barbecued chicken on the unwashed tray that was used to carry the raw chicken from the kitchen. These may appear to be minor oversights, but any one of them could cause serious food poisoning.

Here are some facts to help you make sure the food in your kitchen is kept safe:

MOLD CAN BE AS AWFUL AS IT LOOKS!

Not all molds are harmless! Some produce mycotoxins that can be toxic in small amounts or cause cancer in laboratory animals. Since you can't tell a harmless mold from a harmful one just by looking, you should:

* Buy fresh fruits and vegetables at different stages of ripeness in the quantities you will use.
* Avoid produce with bruises or signs of rot around the stem.
* Never buy food that smells musty—molds could be brewing.
* Avoid nuts that are moldy or discolored. Store nuts in the fridge or, if appropriate, a cool, dry place.
* Don't buy cheese covered with white fuzz or green spots—unless the cheese, for instance Camembert or Roquefort, naturally has them.
* Tightly cover cheese to prevent exposing it to air; mold spores can be carried in the air.
* Save hard cheese that develops mold by cutting away at least an inch (2.5 cm) beyond the mold.
* Don't just scoop mold off the top of liquid or semi-soft foods like jams and jellies; dispose of the entire contents of the jar.
* Never reuse packaging that has been in contact with mold.
* When you dispose of moldy food, make sure children and pets can't get at it.

SALMONELLA—A POTENTIALLY DEADLY POISONING!

The occurrence of salmonella bacteria has been on the increase for some time. It can be found on poultry, meat, fish, eggs, and dairy products. These products do not look or smell odd in any way when they are carrying salmonella, so you have to treat all of them as if they are infected. Here are the rules for handling poultry, the most common carrier of the bacteria. Follow them when handling any potential carrier.

❋ Freeze immediately or refrigerate and use within three days.

❋ Thawing frozen poultry in the refrigerator is the best method; thawing in cold water is also acceptable; if you must thaw at room temperature, wrap the poultry in a heavy paper bag to help prevent the outside from getting warm before the inside thaws.

❋ Scrub hands and utensils that have come in contact with raw poultry extremely well in hot, soapy water. Wash chopping blocks especially carefully and rinse with water and a little bleach—about 2 tablespoons (25 mL) bleach in a quart (1 L) of water will do.

❋ Thorough cooking destroys salmonella; make absolutely sure poultry is cooked through. If you're using a microwave, follow poultry cooking instructions to the letter!

❋ Refrigerate leftover poultry immediately.

❋ Stuffing is an ideal place for bacteria to grow. Consider cooking it in a separate dish. If you do stuff the bird, do it only immediately before cooking and remove the stuffing as soon as you take the bird from the oven.

Watch Out for Cross-Contamination!

Any harmful bacteria or bit of spoiled food can easily contaminate clean food. Wash storage containers thoroughly before reusing. Wash knives and other utensils after they touch any food item. (Never, for instance, chop vegetables you plan to eat raw with a knife you have just used on raw meat or poultry!) Scrub chopping boards and counters very thoroughly after each use; bacteria love to hide in the crevices. Store uncooked meats and poultry in drip-proof dishes at the bottom of your fridge so juices can't drip on other foods, especially ones that will be eaten without cooking. If a little fluid from a raw chicken contaminated with salmonella—as many of them are—drips on an apple, whoever eats the apple can become critically ill.

Health and Welfare Canada now advises against eating raw or undercooked eggs, since some forms of salmonella now grow right inside the egg and are not destroyed by washing the shell. Watch out for things like letting your kids lick the cookie dough spoon if the batter contains eggs!

*Current opinion says that
to prevent bacterial growth, cooked foods should be
refrigerated immediately and not allowed
to cool to room temperature first. Cooked foods
containing any meat, poultry, fish, eggs, or milk products, including
dressings and gravies, should never be left for any more
than two hours at room temperature.*

*However, putting hot foods in the fridge can
lower the fridge's temperature to an unacceptable level and cause
condensation, which, in turn, can cause food to spoil more rapidly.
One solution is to cool foods down quickly
by putting the storage container in cold water and stirring the food
until it's cool. A large amount of leftovers also cools
more quickly if it's divided into
smaller portions.*

For More Information
Check with Health and Welfare Canada's Educational Services
if you have questions about food safety;
they provide free information and detailed brochures
on many specific issues.
Or read:
Safe Food. Michael F. Jacobson, Ph.D., et al.
Venice, Cal.: Living Planet Press, 1991.

BEWARE OF AFLATOXINS!
Aflatoxins are naturally occurring toxins that grow on grains and peanuts. Although their effect on humans is not certain, they are currently considered a carcinogen. To keep your family safe from aflatoxins:

✳ Check peanuts, pecans, walnuts, almonds, Brazil nuts, and pistachios carefully. Dispose of any that are moldy, discolored, or shriveled! If a nut tastes bad, spit it out!

✳ Don't eat sprouted grain if you find any indication of mold.

✳ Although peanut butter companies are supposed to voluntarily monitor for mold growth, tests by *Consumer Reports* (September 1990) found small amounts of aflatoxins in some peanut butters. The article lists results in detail, but in general, the large, national brands tend to be the safest.

CANNING, FREEZING, AND DRYING

In the best of all possible worlds—and kitchens—the cook obtains large quantities of locally grown organic produce when it is in season and preserves it in wholesome, natural ways for use in the winter months.

Unfortunately, preserving and canning bring to mind images of bushels of fruits and vegetables to be chopped, stoves covered with messy, bubbling cauldrons, and counters littered with racks of sterilized jars. But it's not like that at all. Some preserving methods, like freezing, are simple; home canning can become routine after a few tries, and experimenting with old-fashioned methods, like drying, can be fun for the whole family.

Freezing

Quick and convenient, freezing retains color, flavor, texture, and nutrients better than other preserving processes. Although it doesn't kill the micro-organisms that cause spoilage, it slows them down so that many foods can be kept for months. Some types of produce can simply be washed and frozen; others need special treatment before freezing, like blanching or sprinkling with sugar, to stop the action of enzymes, the compounds that cause fruits and vegetables to ripen and eventually decompose. Numerous cookbooks and free government pamphlets tell you exactly how specific fruits and vegetables should be handled. Keep the following guidelines in mind.

Freezing Vegetables

* Vegetables that freeze exceptionally well include asparagus, beans, peas, spinach, whole kernel corn, and mashed squash. Corn on the cob tends to pick up off-flavors unless it's blanched for exactly the right amount of time.

* Vegetables usually eaten raw, such as celery, cucumbers, lettuce, and tomatoes, freeze poorly because of their high moisture content. Lightly cooked tomatoes, however, freeze well for use in sauces.

* Whole beets and raw onions become a bit rubbery when frozen; they are best cut in small pieces.

* Root vegetables, like carrots and parsnips, can be frozen, but they keep more economically in cool storage.

FREEZING TIPS

★ Start with high-quality, firm produce; cut away any bad spots.
★ The very best quality is achieved when produce is processed no more than three hours after picking.
★ Picking produce in the cool morning hours helps prevent wilting.

Freezing Fruit

✳ Fruit needs to be frozen at the peak of maturity—not too green, not too ripe.

✳ Berries, sour cherries, and rhubarb freeze well.

✳ Sweet cherries and pears become too soft when thawed.

✳ Apples, apricots, and peaches discolor unless first treated with ascorbic acid.

✳ Thaw frozen fruit and serve while a few ice crystals still remain.

★ Follow any special instructions on the recipe you're using—or you will end up with discolored or mushy food.
★ Most vegetables require blanching.
★ Blanching causes some vitamin loss, but not as much as can be lost to oxidation when "fresh" vegetables are transported and stored for long periods.
★ Quick blanching at high temperatures followed by immediate cooling causes the least nutrient loss; steam blanching is the best method.
★ Cool vegetables in icy cold water, but leave them in no longer than the blanching time or they'll become waterlogged.
★ All vegetables, except asparagus, fare better when cut into small pieces before blanching.
★ Drain blanched vegetables *thoroughly* before packing.
★ Use reusable containers or packaging; plastic milk bags work exceptionally well and can be reused often. Fill them with water first to make sure there are no tiny holes.
★ Any container or packaging *must* be able to keep moisture in and odors out.
★ Freeze prepared produce as soon as possible, but don't put more in your freezer at once than is recommended in your owner's manual.
★ Labels with dates are invaluable! Use tape and markers specifically made for the job.

Canning

When we speak of canning today, we usually mean preserving food in glass jars. Real home "canning" is possible, too, although it requires a special sealing machine. Canning isn't as difficult as you might imagine, and home-canned foods are safe when prepared according to directions. Care does need to be taken, however. Low-acid foods, including most vegetables, can develop botulism, and other foods can spoil. Don't let this scare you off, though. Proper canning destroys all the micro-organisms that cause these problems.

Before you begin, get a cookbook with thorough directions and recipes for each fruit or vegetable you want to can.

The following points provide you with an overview of canning—including the basic safety precautions—so you can see it's not too hard! And it *is* worth the effort. Every time you open a

jar of succulent peaches in February or hear a guest rave about
your homemade pickles or jams, you'll have the extra satisfaction
of knowing you have saved money and helped the environment.

Canning Hints

★ The equipment you need is very basic: jars that are specifically designed for home canning, a canning kettle with a tight-fitting
lid and rack or wire basket, a wooden spoon, a stainless steel knife,
and the assortment of bowls and colanders you usually have
around the kitchen.

★ For canning vegetables, with the possible exception of tomatoes,
you also need a pressure cooker.

★ Check jars for nicks or cracks; don't use any that are damaged.
(These can, of course, be used for other purposes.)

★ Know what kind of jars you're using! New lids are
needed each time you can for the popular "self-
sealing cap" jars, and new rubber rings are needed for "screw-cap" and "clamp lid" jars. This is
essential!

★ Prepare the number of jars that will fit in your
kettle or cooker. Run them through the dishwasher or wash in hot, soapy water and rinse,
while still hot, with boiling water. Or sterilize
them in a 225° F (110° C) oven for 10 minutes.

★ Prepare lids according to the manufacturer's
instructions.

★ Most fruit is cleaned, cut, and packed tightly,
but without crushing, into sterile jars; boiling syrup
or water, depending on the recipe, is poured over
the fruit; this is called "raw" or "cold packing."

Spring-top

Gem

Mason

★ Most vegetables and a few fruits are cleaned and
cooked first, packed into jars, and covered with
the cooking liquid; this is "hot packing."

★ Follow your recipe and leave the proper space at the top of
the jar; usually one inch (2.5 cm) for starchy vegetables like
corn, peas, and beans, and half that for most other fruits and
vegetables.

★ Once your liquid is added, get rid of air bubbles by running a
sterile knife around the inside of the jars.

★ Wipe the necks of the jars completely clean with a sterile cloth.

★ Put on the scalded lids. Follow the directions dictated by the
type of lid: pour boiling water over self-sealing lids; turn rubber
ring lids a quarter-turn; and close—but don't clamp—clamp-
type lids.

★ Process immediately! Follow your recipe and instructions exactly and process your filled jars in a boiling water bath or a pressure cooker as directed.

★ Always process a full load. Use extra jars filled with water to
take up space if needed.

★ In the boiling water bath, jars *must* be covered by at least 2 in

(5 cm) of water. Start timing once water has reached a rolling boil. Keep the water boiling; add more boiling water if needed.

★ For pressure canning, follow the exact instructions in your owner's manual or in a recipe for your type of pressure cooker. Do not start timing before the proper pressure is reached. If you have a gauge dial on your pressure cooker, be positive it's accurate. Regulate the heat to keep the pressure constant. When the time is up, let the pressure return to zero on its own. Follow normal precautions for opening your cooker.

★ Remove jars and place them, well separated, on wood, Formica, wire racks, or folded towels. Avoid cold surfaces and drafts.

★ As soon as bubbling in the jars stops, clamp down clamp lids or tighten screw caps. Don't screw lids too tight or you'll stretch the rubber and ruin the seal.

★ To be extra-safe when using home-canned foods:
- Always check jars for signs of spoilage: bulging lids, foaming, mold, or discoloration.
- Cloudiness or excessive liquid loss may also indicate spoilage.
- Smell contents for strange or "off" odors.
- The food should not be any softer or mushier than commercially canned foods would be.
- Immediately destroy any food that appears to be tainted.
- Always bring all home-canned vegetables to a boil and simmer for 10 minutes before tasting them. If they foam or smell odd, dump them in the compost bin (or flush them down the toilet).

> **Sugarless Preserves**
> Most recipes for making jam and many for preserving fruits call for sugar. If you'd prefer an alternative, read Putting It Up With Honey, by Susan Geiskopf (Oregon: Quicksilver Productions, 1979).

Storage the Natural Way

With all this emphasis on freezing and canning, we shouldn't forget that people were storing food for centuries before electricity was discovered. Many of those old methods are viable today, and most are environment-friendly: they get the required energy directly from nature.

SOLAR DRYING

Drying is one of the oldest methods of preserving food. In principle, it is extremely simple. Removing moisture retards the growth of micro-organisms that require water and increases the percentage of acid in acidic foods like fruits, which slows down the action of enzymes. Low-acid vegetables need to be blanched, just as they do for canning and freezing, to stop the growth of enzymes.

Although electric food dryers exist, solar drying is far more environmentally sound. It also has a satisfying, cyclic rhythm to it: sun and water give the food life, then the sun removes the water and lengthens the food's life.

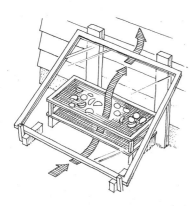

Solar drying can be done, especially in hot, dry climates, by simply spreading cleaned and chopped produce on a screen and placing it in the sun. In moister, cooler climates where the produce is likely to spoil or become infested before the sun can do its work, a solar dryer speeds the process along.

Several books contain plans for building a solar dryer; check your library. Some require a bit of carpentry work, others are as simple as laying a screen on a few bricks against a south wall and propping a storm window at an angle over the top.

Solar dryers are more versatile than you might think. Fruit leathers, fruit butters, and even ketchup can be made with them!

COOL AND COLD STORAGE

When you're thinking of ways to store your bountiful harvests, don't forget the techniques used by your grandparents and great-grandparents. They took advantage of the cool outside air that nature so conveniently provides right after harvest time to store their home-grown produce—and you can do the same today. Most houses have a space that can be used for natural cold storage. The old-fashioned root cellar is ideal for this, but a basement, tool-shed, closed-in porch, spare room, or apartment balcony can be used. The idea of cold storage is to keep food cold without freezing it, so containers need to be insulated if the temperature in your storage space will drop below freezing.

Another time-honored storage technique is to leave root vegetables right in the ground. Carrots, parsnips, radishes, and kale covered with a thick layer of straw or mulch can be kept through frost and snow—and dug up when they are needed.

Earth mounds were also popular in earlier days. They are very simple to make and are viable in any climate where the average winter temperature doesn't go much below 30° F (–1° C).

Another old-fashioned yet ingenious cooling technique was the evaporation box. You can make one out of an orange crate or a box frame. Make the storage shelves from chicken wire or well-spaced wood slats and cover the box with burlap. Place part of the burlap in water. The moisture will eventually spread around the whole box. Air circulation carries the moisture away and creates the same cooling effect you feel on your skin when you climb out of a swimming pool on a hot summer day.

If you are interested in learning more about these and other natural storage methods, such as spring water cooling houses and old-fashioned ice boxes, you can find a wealth of information in your library. Be sure to look for *Home Food Systems* by Roger B. Yepsen (Emmaus, Phil.: Rodale Press, 1981).

BOOKS!

The Busy Person's Guide to Preserving Food. Janet Bachand Chadwick. Charlotte, Vermont: Garden Way Publishing, 1982.

Seasonal Freezer Cookbook. Caroline Ellwood, et al. London: Octopus Books, 1983.

Keeping the Harvest: Home Storage of Fruits and Vegetables. Nancy Thurber and Gretchen Mead. Charlotte, Vermont: Garden Way Publishing, 1982.

KIDS IN THE KITCHEN

Many children today are even more concerned about the environment than adults are. To keep this concern from becoming overwhelming, adults need to help children focus on the many things they can do to help. The kitchen provides countless opportunities to do just that. It's the perfect place to get kids involved in the Three R's and to show them how important it is not to waste. Here is only a small sample of the fun kitchen activities you and your kids can do together. Check children's science and activity books in your local library for many more.

MAKING GLUE FROM MILK

Next time you have some skim milk that's on the verge of going bad, don't dump it down the drain—make glue instead! Here's how:

1. Put 2 cups (500 mL) skim milk into a glass or enamel-coated saucepan, and add 6 Tbsp (90 mL) vinegar. Warm the mixture slowly, stirring constantly. (Note: You *must* use skim milk.)
2. When the milk begins to curdle, remove it from the heat but keep stirring. When the curdling stops, strain off the liquid—or whey—completely and save the curds.
3. Mix together 1/4 cup (50 mL) water and 1 Tbsp (15 mL) baking soda. Add mixture to the curds. Stir—and you have your glue! Color it with food coloring if desired, and store in a tightly sealed container.

Adapted from *Mr. Wizard's Experiments for Young Scientists*, by Don Herbert. Garden City, NY: Doubleday, 1959.

HOMEMADE DYES AND COLORINGS

Kids get a kick out of making dyes from things you might otherwise compost or throw out—like onion skins, shriveled beets, or wilted spinach. The dyes can be used to color homemade paints and modeling clays. (Use the following recipe for play dough or find others in the arts and crafts section of your library.)

Chop the vegetable matter into small pieces, cover with water, bring to a boil, and simmer for about half an hour. Strain, and store liquid in an airtight container for a few days. Freeze for longer storage. To make:

Yellow   Save onion skins until you have enough to fill a pot.

Yellow-green Use carrot tops.

Red   Use beets or red cabbage.

Blue   Use blueberries; simmer only for about 15 minutes.

Brown   Use used teabags.

Homemade Play Dough

Homemade play dough is a good alternative to the heavily packaged commercial varieties. It's also a terrific money-saver! Your library has countless recipes for homemade clay and play dough. Here is one that has a very smooth texture, can be colored with food coloring, and keeps for months in an airtight container in the fridge. Since homemade dyes may spoil in time, they are best used for dough that is to be modeled and dried fairly soon.

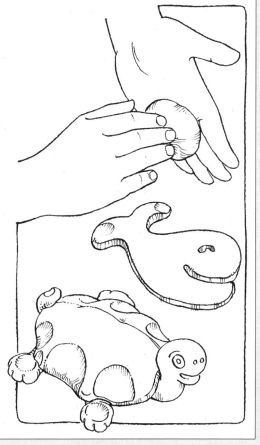

1/2 cup	salt	125 mL
1 cup	flour	250 mL
2 Tbsp	cream of tartar	25 mL
2 Tbsp	oil	25 mL
1 cup	water	250 mL

In a thick-bottomed saucepan, mix together well the salt, flour, and cream of tartar. Add oil and water. Cook over moderate heat, stirring constantly, until the mixture is quite thick. Remove from heat and let cool. Knead dough until it is smooth. Knead in coloring if desired.

GROW THAT GARBAGE!

The kitchen is a gold mine of things to grow indoors. You can grow a luxurious vine as tall as a person from an old sweet potato, or an indoor tree from an avocado pit. Poke a few toothpicks in the sides of the potato or pit to form supports, and soak the lower half of the potato or pit in a glass of water until it sprouts. Then plant it in a flower pot—and watch it grow!

You can turn many other bits of potential garbage into greenery: you can plant the tops of carrots, turnips, parsnips, beets, and pineapples. Just trim the tops—including about a half to one inch (3 to 5 cm) of the actual vegetable—and plant them in a pot of soil with part of the top showing.

Try planting dried beans, dried whole peas, and popcorn, too. Even raw peanuts can be planted to make attractive plants. Just take them out of the shell and soak them for a day before you plant them!

Turn Garbage into Jewelry!

Carrot Necklace
Peel some old carrots and cut them into rounds about 1/4 inch (5 mm) thick. String the pieces with a needle and a piece of double thread. When you've finished, make sure the necklace is long enough to fit around your head. Then tie the ends together. Hang the necklace in a dry place for about ten days, and you will have a colorful—and unusual—creation.

Seed Necklaces and Bracelets
Many seeds can be used to make interesting jewelry. The ones from pumpkins, canteloupes, and honeydew melons work well. Wash them well, place them in bowls, and cover them with food coloring or natural dyes. Let them soak overnight. Rinse the seeds well in a sieve and pat them dry. Use them to make bracelets and necklaces just as you would with carrots.

CAUTION FOR PARENTS: Don't let your children use pits from apricots, peaches, plums, or cherries for jewelry—they can be toxic. And don't use seeds or berries from wild or yard plants unless you are *absolutely* sure they are safe—a surprising number are poisonous.

CHAPTER FIVE

KEEPING IT CLEAN AND GREEN

If you haven't yet been introduced to environment-friendly cleaning, and you're thinking you'll never be able to get your kitchen really clean without the arsenal of heavy-duty commercial cleaners you have under your sink, don't despair. You *can* get your kitchen just as clean using substances that are far less harmful to the environment.

Many commercial cleaners, disinfectants, and polishes contain hazardous chemicals that contribute to pollution, first when they are manufactured and later when they are washed down our drains into our waterways or thrown into dumps where they can seep into groundwater and leak into the air. These products' acrid fumes can contribute to indoor pollution and, in some cases, be harmful to our health.

When choosing cleaning products for the green kitchen, select from the environmentally friendlier products available from health food stores, co-ops, and independent salespeople. You can find "green" cleaning products in some supermarkets, but read the labels carefully to make sure they are *really* environment-friendly. (See the section on labels, "Greenspeak or Really Green," in Chapter Two.) Another alternative is to make your own.

Homemade cleaners can be substituted for almost any commercial product. These do-it-yourself alternatives are not only safer for the environment, they are also much easier on your pocketbook.

EASIER GREEN CLEANING

It can't be denied that elbow grease is a necessary ingredient in green cleaning. Simple physical action—wiping, mopping, sweeping, and scrubbing—is as important as any complex chemical reaction when it comes to getting rid of dirt. Still, green cleaning doesn't have to be drudgery, and it is probably much easier than you expect. Many environmentally safe, alternative cleaning products do an excellent job. Whether you buy these products or make your own, here are a few tricks that make green cleaning easier:

- Clean spills and messes immediately and, in general, clean often. Dried, hardened, and baked-on grime is almost always harder to clean off.
- Use the two-bucket method for big jobs like cleaning floors. Keep your diluted cleaner in one bucket and clean water in the other. Dip your sponge into your cleaning solution and do a bit of cleaning. Rinse the sponge in the water bucket, wipe the cleaned area, and again squeeze the sponge into the water bucket. Change the water as needed. Your cleaning solution stays full-strength longer and does a much better job because it doesn't get mixed with grime.
- Always sweep, dust, or vacuum to get rid of surface dirt before you apply liquid cleaners.
- You don't want to be wasteful, but you have to use enough homemade cleaner to get the job done. Experiment to find the quantity of cleaner that works best—and don't be stingy.
- Let your cleaner sit for a while after you have applied it so that the dissolving action can do some of your work for you. Homemade and organic cleaners sometimes take a little more time to work than their heavy-duty counterparts.
- Remove the mushy dissolved dirt with a sponge, clean rag, or squeegee and rinse the area well if necessary. Although some commercial cleaners don't require rinsing, most homemade ones do.

Don't try to become a home chemist! It could be dangerous. Never mix commercially prepared cleaners. Mix the seven basic cleaners listed in this chapter only according to recipes from trusted sources.

NEVER MIX AMMONIA WITH CHLORINE BLEACH. THE MIXTURE CREATES A POISONOUS GAS! Many commercially prepared cleaners contain one or the other. For instance, many scouring powders contain chlorine and many window cleaners contain ammonia.

The Four Basic Safer Cleaners

Most kitchen cleaning jobs can be handled with four safe, inexpensive, everyday items: baking soda, cornstarch, pure soap, and vinegar.

- **Vinegar** (5% acetic acid)
  cleans, deodorizes, and removes mildew, calcium crusts, stains, and wax buildup. It is a mild disinfectant and is mildly corrosive.
- **Baking Soda** (sodium bicarbonate)
  is the champion kitchen cleaner. It cleans, deodorizes, scours, polishes, and removes stains.
- **Pure Soap**
  can be used to clean just about everything, but it must be rinsed off so that it doesn't leave a film.
- **Cornstarch**
  is an odorless pure vegetable powder. Use it to wash windows, freshen carpets, and clean up greasy spills.

It's hard to believe, but not all vinegar—simple, diluted acetic acid—comes from sources that are as "natural" as we might think. Cider, apple, malt, wine, and other tasty, trendy vinegars are all made from fermented fruits or grains. But some white vinegars are now made from petroleum products instead of the traditional grain mash.

While any vinegar that is sold as "food" is safe to eat and harmless to the environment, the process of creating white vinegar from petroleum uses greater amounts of energy and consumes a non- renewable resource.

You can tell if you're getting a white vinegar made from natural grain mash by reading the label. Manufacturers are required to tell you if their source was grain mash—they are not required to tell you if it was petroleum!

THREE CLEANERS FOR TOUGHER JOBS

Three other acceptable cleaning materials are washing soda, borax, and household ammonia. These compounds are toxic in varying degrees; they should be used with moderation and caution. Wear gloves and use only in well-ventilated areas. Keep them out of the reach of children.

- **Washing Soda** (sodium carbonate)
  softens water and can be added to the washing machine to help clean clothes. It is moderately toxic and can irritate mucous membranes.
- **Borax** (sodium borate)
  eliminates odors, helps control molds, and works as a mild disinfectant. It can irritate the eyes, nose, and throat.
- **Household Ammonia**
  cleans, deodorizes, and disinfects; it cleans ovens, grills, and tiles and removes floor wax. It is a strong alkaline that can burn the skin, eyes, nose, and throat; even the fumes can cause headache, nausea, and chest pain.

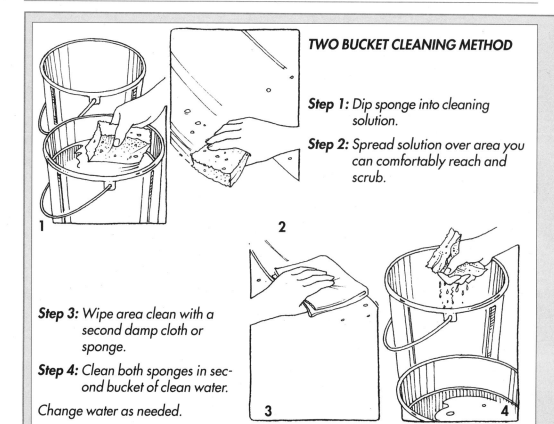

TWO BUCKET CLEANING METHOD

Step 1: Dip sponge into cleaning solution.

Step 2: Spread solution over area you can comfortably reach and scrub.

Step 3: Wipe area clean with a second damp cloth or sponge.

Step 4: Clean both sponges in second bucket of clean water.

Change water as needed.

Simple Cleaner
1/4 cup (50 mL) pure soap
2 gal (8 L) hot water
For less demanding jobs, like regular floor washing and countertop cleaning, this works well. Be sure to rinse the soap film away. A splash of vinegar in the rinse water makes this easier. For a fresh scent, add 1/4 cup (50 mL) lemon juice to the soap mixture. Another simple cleaner can be made with the same quantities of hot water and washing soda.

All-Purpose Cleaner
1/2 cup (125 mL) pure soap
1/4 cup (50 mL) borax
1 drop eucalyptus oil
4 qt (4 L) hot water
Mix the ingredients thoroughly. Use the mixture to clean bathroom fixtures, countertops, tiles, floors, and painted walls. Rinse with clean water after washing.

Wall and Floor Tile Cleaner
1/2 cup (125 mL) shredded coarse soap
1/2 cup (125 mL) washing soda
4 qt (4 L) hot water
Dissolve the ingredients in the hot water. Scrub the cleaner onto tiles with a stiff brush, and rinse well.

Drain Cleaner

1/2 cup (125 mL) baking soda
1/4 cup (50 mL) vinegar
1 kettle boiling water

Pour the baking soda down the drain, then pour in the vinegar. Wait about 15 minutes, while the mixture fizzes. Some sources recommend putting the plug in the sink to force the fizzing action downward. Next pour the boiling water directly into the drain. Use this recipe regularly to prevent serious clogging and keep your kitchen drains smelling fresh. But don't forget to focus on prevention: use traps to keep bits of matter from flowing down the drains and never pour grease into your sink. If your drains do become seriously clogged, try an old-fashioned plunger!

Note that other homemade cleaners calling for baking soda and vinegar are not much good, as the two compounds neutralize—or cancel each other out—in the initial fizzing reaction.

Descalers

One part white vinegar
Two parts water

Removing the mineral deposits that build up in appliances will keep them working much more efficiently. Use this simple solution as a descaler instead of buying the expensive commercial ones:

* Kettles—pour in the solution, bring it to a boil, then rinse well.

* Coffee makers—pour the solution into the water reservoir and run the coffee maker through a regular cycle as if you were making coffee. Repeat the process once or twice with plain water.

* Irons—pour in the solution, let it stand for 30 minutes, then rinse thoroughly.

Oven Cleaner

2 Tbsp (25 mL) dishwashing soap
1 Tbsp (15 mL) borax
1 qt (1 L) warm water

Mix together in a plastic spray bottle. Spray on dirty surfaces and leave for 20 minutes. Wipe thoroughly. Use a plastic scraper or reusable scrubber on stubborn spots.

A less toxic option is to sprinkle your oven bottom first with water, then with baking soda. Let it sit overnight. A good deal of wiping is needed to get out all the baking soda.

Although these are good alternatives to caustic commercial oven cleaners, the best is prevention. Use a second pan or liner to catch drips, and wipe up spills as soon as the oven is cool with a little baking soda on a wet cloth. Try cleaning bigger spills by sprinkling them with salt while the oven is still hot; when the oven cools, many spills will lift right off.

Most homemade cleaners work better when they are fresh, so make up only as much as you need each time. If you have some leftover or have made up a recipe that is said to keep well, store the mixtures in unbreakable containers preferably with child-proof lids. Keep them out of the reach of children just as you would commercial cleaners. And make sure *all* ingredients are listed on the containers—not just so you know what's in them but in case you need to provide the information in an emergency.

INDOOR AIR POLLUTION

Even in the dirtiest city, the air inside your home usually contains five to ten times more pollution than the air just outside the window. One reason for this is poor ventilation; not enough fresh air gets into today's tightly sealed and insulated buildings. The other cause of indoor air pollution is the hundreds of toxic materials we use to build, decorate, and clean our homes.

BEFORE

Wood window and door frames are often treated with poisonous insecticides, mildewcides, or fungicides that can out-gas for years.

Urea formaldehyde foam insulation (or UFFI) in your walls releases formaldehyde gas. The fiber particles from other types of insulation, if released, can irritate the eyes, nose, and throat, and cause allergies and respiratory disease.

Old paint often contains lead. If children swallow flakes of paint, the lead can permanently impair their mental and physical development.

Lead may have been used to solder the pipes that carry your drinking water.

The demand for ebony, mahogany, rosewood, teak, and other tropical hardwoods and veneers for cabinets and trim is one of the reasons for the destruction of the rainforests.

The plywood, fiber board, or particle board used to make your kitchen cabinets slowly releases formaldehyde from the glues that hold it together. This irritating gas can cause coughing, fatigue, skin rashes, severe allergic reaction, and even cancer.

Carbon monoxide (CO), a product of incomplete combustion, can be produced by furnaces, ranges, and wood stoves. High levels of CO can incapacitate and kill. Nitrogen oxides, another combustion by-product, can irritate the eyes, nose, and throat, and cause respiratory infections in young children.

Many vinyl floor tiles contain asbestos. When the tiles are cut or damaged, they may release dangerous asbestos fibers into the air. Soft vinyl tiles contain more volatile plasticizers than hard vinyl.

The solvents used in many glues, sealants, caulking compounds, and oil-based paints can damage the central nervous system, liver, and kidneys. Some solvents have been linked to cancer.

Unless you're one of the three pigs, your home isn't made of just bricks and sticks and straw. Irritating chemicals can be released or "out-gassed" into the air by many common building materials, including floor tiles, carpeting, caulking, paints and finishes, paneling and plywood, glues, and wood preservatives. Although we usually can't smell them, dangerous pollutants may continue to leak out of the floors, walls, and cabinets for years.

AFTER

Glass doors and shelves do not release toxic gases. Use epoxy resins (which are relatively non-toxic when fully cured) rather than formaldehyde-containing glues. White glue and carpenter's yellow glue are also safer.

For carpets and drapes, stick to untreated wool, cotton, linen, or other natural fibers. Wooden shutters may be an environment-friendly alternative.

Install a range hood to blow hot gases outside (not just into the attic). Make sure all exhaust vents are set well away from windows, doors, and air-intake vents. There is no point in sucking the dirty air straight back into the house.

Seal wood counters with tung oil or mineral oil.

Install stainless steel, stone, or solid plastic counters around sinks, where water could damage wood countertops.

Install ceramic tiles or hardwood floors.

Instead of plywood, use solid dimensional lumber, such as two-by-fours and planking, or metal cabinets. If you do use plywood, buy exterior grades, which do not release as much formaldehyde gas. And paint over all exposed surfaces, including the ends and undersides, with special environmental sealers. (Latex paint won't seal plywood.)

For counters and floors, use local hardwoods like maple, cherry, oak, alder, apple, aspen, beech, birch, elm, hickory, and black walnut. Useful softwoods include pine, spruce, hemlock, and Douglas-fir.

Use non-toxic adhesives to lay carpets, and ventilate the area for several days after installation.

Generally, latex (water- or milk-based) paints and plant-oil and wood-oil based paints contain fewer solvents and other dangerous chemicals than oil-based paints and enamels. In addition, they do not require strong solvents and thinners for cleanup.

KITCHEN WONDER WORKERS

Vinegar

* Add to the dishwashing water for especially greasy or smelly items.

* Use equal amounts of salt and vinegar to clean coffee and tea stains from cups.

* Pour some vinegar on a piece of bread and leave it overnight in lunchboxes or plastic storage containers to get rid of smells.

* Rub a little on your hands before and after cutting onions to get rid of smells. It also removes fruit stains from your fingers.

* Pour a little into a glass jar and let it sit to remove smells.

* Dampen a cloth with some and use it to remove spots from stainless steel.

* Use it to remove food stains or discolorations from the inside of cookware, including non-stick. Pour the solution in the pot and let it soak for 30 minutes. For tough discolorations on aluminum, mix cream of tartar with the vinegar, add to 2 or 3 Tbsp (25 to 50 mL) to 1 qt (1 L) of water and simmer.

* Mix it with salt and simmer to remove charred food from your cast iron pans or skillets.

* Pour it onto a rag and drape it for a while on faucets or taps to clean off lime and soap.

* Prevent mildew in your fridge by wiping the inside down with vinegar after cleaning.

Baking Soda

* Use with water to clean coffee, tea, and juice stains off kitchen counters. Scrub it in, leave for 30 minutes, then wipe up well.

* Use with hot water to clean and deodorize the inside of the refrigerator.

* Tear the lid off a box and leave it in the refrigerator to absorb smells. When it loses its power, use it for cleaning.

* Throw a handful in the bottom of your dishwasher in the morning before you put in the first dishes. It will absorb odors until you run the machine after the evening meal.

* Rub it into your hands with a little water to remove onion, garlic, and other strong food smells.

* Use it to scrub your chopping board to remove onion and other odors.

* Use it to clean glass, porcelain enamel, and metal cookware without scratching.

* Sprinkle dry or use a paste (3 parts baking soda to 1 part water) to scrub off burned or baked-on food. For tough jobs, sprinkle it liberally on the bottom of the pan, add a couple of cups (about 500 mL) of water, simmer for a while, then let the mixture stand for a few hours. Often you can then pick the burned material right out of the pot. To save heat, start the process while the pan is still hot.

* Use it to remove stains from your coffee or tea pots.

* Use it dry or in a soaking solution to freshen coolers, Thermoses, and plastic containers. It also remove stubborn smells from clay cookware.

* Keep a container of baking soda near the stove to toss on grease, oil, or electrical fires. But don't throw it into a deep-fat fryer; it could cause the grease to splatter and the fire to spread.

Dishwasher Efficiency

Environmentalists have conflicting opinions about dishwashers. As we explained in Chapter One, washing one full load of dishes at the end of the day in the dishwasher *can* use less hot and cold water than hand-washing dishes after every meal. Of course, hand-washing is more energy-efficient if you are careful about water consumption and do not wash or rinse under running water.

To be efficient, your dishwasher must have a good Energuide rating and a heat booster or "sani" setting. Without the booster you need to turn your household's water heater up to 140° F (60° C) —a real waste of energy. Dishwashers use about 310 to 520 gal (1200 to 2000 L) of water and 100 kWh of energy a month. If you choose to use a dishwasher, keep the following in mind:

- Use your dishwasher only when you have a full load.
- Use the short "econo" cycle when you can; it uses less water and energy than the heavy-duty cycle.
- Rinsing the dishes before loading will keep food from drying on and let you use the econo cycle more often. To be more conservative with the rinsing water, use a damp cloth and wipe the food right into the composting bin.
- *Always* air dry the dishes. One estimate says air drying can cut dishwasher energy use by 45%.
- If your machine doesn't have a switch for choosing "air dry," just switch it off when the drying cycle begins.
- Dishes will dry with the door open or shut. Opening the door can add heat and needed humidity to your kitchen in the winter.
- Avoid the "plate warmer" cycle. Instead, use leftover oven heat to warm the plates.
- You may be able to cut down on the amount of detergent you use; find out how hard the water is in your area by calling the city water department or regional agricultural agent, then check in your operating manual to see how much detergent is required for that type of water—or just experiment to discover the smallest effective amount. The softer the water, the less detergent you'll need.

DISHWASHER DETERGENTS
Several companies, such as The Soap Factory, make phosphate-free dishwasher detergent. Many commercial products contain higher percentages of phosphates than laundry detergents do. In the U.S. the percentage of phosphate may be over 5%, and in Canada a number of products are over 25%. Dishwashers also use more detergent than would be used if you washed by hand.

KILL GERMS ON CONTACT!

Television commercials have convinced us that we need to do a lot of disinfecting around the home. But even the disinfectants that are advertised to "kill germs on contact" don't kill all germs. To *sterilize* something—like a baby bottle—you need to immerse it in boiling drinking water for three to five minutes. Soap and/or baking soda and hot water are not disinfectants, but they keep your kitchen *clean*, and they do wash away many germs.

Vinegar is a mild disinfectant, borax a somewhat stronger one. One hospital experimented with a solution of 1/2 cup (125 mL) borax to 1 gal (4 L) hot water for general cleaning. They monitored bacteria counts for a year and found the solution met their germicidal requirements.

One of the few kitchen items that actually needs to be disinfected is a cutting board, or a counter, that has come in contact with raw poultry. Washing with hot, soapy water and rinsing with water and bleach is recommended to kill salmonella bacteria.

KITCHEN-CLEANING HINTS

★ Simmer a little vinegar or lemon peel in water on the stove to remove most cooking odors. Or simmer a few cloves and a little cinnamon to fill the kitchen with a spicy scent. Baking apples with cinnamon does the same thing, and you can eat them afterwards!

★ Cleaning windows with vinegar and water is an old standby. If it doesn't work well in your kitchen, try ammonia and water instead. Ammonia is alkaline; vinegar is acidic—they work on different kinds of dirt. Mix 1/4 cup (50 mL) ammonia and 2 cups (500 mL) water in a spray bottle; the cleaner will do everything a commercial glass cleaner does—and will save you a lot of money!

★ Clean woodwork with cold tea or Murphy's Oil Soap. Don't use ammonia on wood. It can ruin the finish over time.

★ A few tablespoons of vinegar in the rinse water will prevent spots on washed dishes.

★ To clean appliance surfaces, combine 2 cups (500 mL) very hot water, 2 Tbsp (25 mL) vinegar, 1 tsp (5 mL) borax, and 1/4 tsp (1 mL) liquid soap in a spray bottle. Shake until the borax has dissolved, then spray on and wipe off.

★ Keep a little talcum powder in the kitchen to sprinkle on grease spots on your clothes. Leave it for about 30 minutes and brush it off. The grease usually goes too!

★ Use soda water to clean many kitchen rug stains. Rub it in immediately, wait a while, and sponge it off. It's also good for removing chocolate stains from clothes.

★ Take black heel or crayon marks off the kitchen linoleum by rubbing with a damp cloth and toothpaste.

★ Keep stainless steel shiny by rubbing it with lemon peel before washing.

★ For crystal that sparkles, wash it in warm water and a little ammonia. Or use white vinegar in the rinse water—about a cup (250 mL) to a sink full of water.

★ Pour salt immediately on red wine spilled on your tablecloth or clothes; launder as usual. It works on rugs, too; vacuum when dry.

★ To clean the grates from your grill or the removable rings and drip pans from your stove, place them in a plastic garbage bag—one without any holes—and pour in a cup (250 mL) of ammonia. Tie it tightly and leave outside or in a laundry sink overnight. Carefully open the bag in the morning—the fumes will be very strong. Wash the items in hot, soapy water. They should come just as clean as they would have with oven cleaner.

★ Remove the odor from a spice mill by grinding uncooked rice.

★ Reuse those plastic grape and onion bags. Turn them into dish scrubbers by tying them around a sponge or dishcloth. Or fill them with leftover slivers of pure soap to make an excellent sink scrubber.

★ Use ketchup to remove tarnish from a copper pot, or soak stained copper bottoms in sour milk for about an hour, then wash as usual.

KITCHEN PEST CONTROL

You might find it hard to believe—especially when you see a cockroach scurry across your kitchen floor—but every creature has its place in the scheme of things. Roaches, for example, help decompose the refuse of life; household centipedes eat flies; spiders help keep the general population of insects down.

We are so used to thinking of all insects as "pests" that it has become difficult for us to remember that many are extremely beneficial and others perfectly harmless. This—along with a great deal of advertising—has made us believe that we need to wage a non-stop deadly war on insects. According to Debra Lynn Dadd in *Nontoxic, Natural, and Earthwise*, suburban homeowners in the United States use more pesticides per acre than farmers do in their fields!

Pesticides can be harmful to much more than bugs. Household pesticides are the number-two cause of poisonings in the home. Accidental inhalation or contact with some pesticides or their residues can cause a wide range of complaints, including skin or eye irritation, dizziness, nausea, numbness, and headaches.

This doesn't mean you have to let cockroaches or any pest take control of your kitchen! Although cockroaches aren't harmful—they're merely unpleasant-looking creatures—some pests can be poisonous or carry diseases. Still, try not to forget that insects are an important part of the ecological system. Try to prevent infestations before they occur. If they do occur, make every effort to repel the pests instead of killing them. If you are determined to kill them, choose the most humane and natural method possible.

HERE ARE SOME BASIC GUIDELINES FOR PREVENTIVE PEST CONTROL:

* Make your kitchen an unpleasant place for pests to live. Make sure there is neither food nor water for them.
* Keep your kitchen very clean. Wipe up crumbs and spills immediately.
* Wipe jars before putting them back in the cupboard.
* Keep all cupboard foods in sturdy, tightly sealed containers.
* Make sure all food containers are clean before putting them in the recycling box.
* Keep compost scraps in a thick, well-closed container; empty them often and rinse the container with vinegar.
* Fix leaky taps, pipes, sink rime, or any other source of little water puddles. (A pet's water bowl or food dish may even be the cause of a persistent problem.)
* Try to discover where pests are entering your home and plug the place of entry with plaster, wood, steel wool, or other solid or inpenetrable material.
* Place a natural deterrent—such as lemon peel for ants—near the place of entry. Some natural deterrents, like mint for mice, can be grown outside. Library books list such natural deterrents and repellents.
* Clean up the clutter that pests like to hide in, particularly the kind that tends to become permanent in basements, attics, or the corners of closets.

Ants
- It's especially important to keep your kitchen clean if you want to avoid ants; once they find a food supply, they go back and fetch their friends.
- Check for cracks in walls and foundations that could be entry points.
- Natural deterrents include planting mint or tansy (a very invasive herb!) or placing lemon juice, lemon peels, cayenne pepper, vinegar, or cucumber peels near the entry points.

Flies
- Put screens on all windows and doors and keep them in good repair.
- Keep garbage cans and compost buckets tightly closed and very clean.
- Keep your yard and litter box free of pet feces.
- Tie a bundle of cloves in cheesecloth and hang them in the room or along the sides of frequently used doors.
- Scratch the rind of an orange and leave the fruit out in the room. Flies are repelled by citrus oil.
- Wash down picnic tables with a mild solution of bleach and water before and after eating. Flies seem to hate the smell of chlorine.

Weevils, beetles, and other food-storage pests
- To capture beetles, set an empty jar on top of them and slide a stiff piece of paper under the opening. Set them free away from the house.
- Keep all containers of grain products clean and tightly closed. Store them in the fridge if possible.
- Put a bay leaf in each container.
- Make small bags of peppercorns with cheesecloth and hang them in food storage bins.

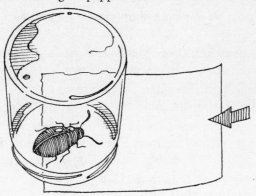

Cockroaches
- Scrub infested areas extremely thoroughly. Repeat frequently, until you are sure the roaches are gone.
- Place natural deterrents such as bay leaves, cayenne pepper, cucumber peels, or cucumber peels sprinkled with cayenne near entry points or infested areas.

Mosquitoes

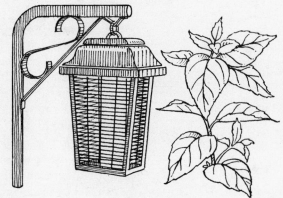

- Put screens on all windows and doors and keep them in good repair. A mosquito can get through a very little hole.
- Plant basil in outdoor windowboxes or indoor herb gardens near your windows.
- Make sure your yard doesn't contain any stagnant water that would serve as a mosquito breeding ground. Keep water fresh or moving in things like bird baths and decorative ponds.
- Burn oil of citronella candles or yard torches.

Moths

- Always clean garments before storing and keep them in airtight containers.
- Store clothes with a natural moth deterrent such as oil of cedar, cedar chips, or whole peppercorns.
- Place sachets in your drawers or closets; make them out of cotton, linen, or silk cloth filled with either dried lavender or equal amounts of dried mint and rosemary.

Mice

- Make sure there is no food available for them; keep cereals, pasta, flours, and grains in strong, tightly lidded containers instead of the cardboard or plastic.
- Eliminate hiding places by getting rid of clutter.
- Spot possible entry points by following trails of mouse droppings; plug these holes well.

Spiders

- Remember that spiders are very beneficial in the home, as they keep the populations of other insects down.
- Use library books to familiarize yourself with the types of spiders in your area. You will then see how many are harmless and learn to recognize the few that are poisonous and how they should be dealt with.
- Use a jar and stiff paper to remove harmless spiders (*see* Weevils).
- Vacuum up egg sacs before they get a chance to hatch.

COMPOSTING

No green kitchen is complete without a composting bucket of one sort or another. If you think composting isn't worth the trouble, here's a fact that should change your mind: An average North American family that does *not* compost annually throws away the amount of iron in 500 eggs, protein in 60 steaks, and vitamins in 95 glasses of orange juice—just in potato peelings!

Composting is simply the process of allowing nature to break down the energy and nutrients stored in organic matter so that it can all be used again. When you use compost on your garden, the precious nutrients they once contained are returned to you in the form of next year's vegetables. Of course if you don't have a vegetable garden, you can still feed compost to your flowerbeds, bushes, grass, trees, houseplants, and windowboxes, and avoid the use of commercial fertilizers. If you live in an apartment, you can easily compost on your balcony. Use the results on your houseplants or balcony flowerboxes, or donate it to your apartment building's grounds.

Composting Is Easy!

Look around a wooded area on a fall day and you'll see how easy composting can be. The leaves fall from the trees, break down over the winter, and feed the soil in the spring. If the tree in your backyard can do it, you can too!

Getting Worms to Do the Work

One of the latest, and most interesting, concepts in composting is called vermicomposting—a process in which a species of hungry worms nibble away at your kitchen scraps and rapidly turn them into usable vermicompost. Vermicompost is to worms what manure is to cows!

A thousand tiny red wigglers—the favored species—can eat more than 4 lb (2 kg) of vegetable scraps a week.

Home vermicomposting systems can be built with basic carpentry skills, or you can purchase small kitchen units that are ideal for apartments.

Although vermicomposting is easy, read up on it before you begin. Your local library should have plenty of information. It is well worth the effort, especially if you have children. They are fascinated with vermicomposting, and it makes an excellent family project.

COMPOSTING TIPS

Most common composting worries are easily remedied. The solutions to almost any specific problem can be found in your library. Here are a few hints that should cover most basic concerns:

❊ To start your compost, put down a layer of coarse material—small branches, shrub trimmings, grass clippings, etc. Add a layer of rich garden soil, rotted manure, or seaweed so the proper bacteria are present. Begin adding your kitchen waste: fruit and vegetable trimmings, egg shells, tea leaves, and coffee grounds. Even small bits of paper, like teabags, are fine.

❊ If you don't want your compost pile to attract animals, avoid bones, meat and fish scraps, fat and oil, eggs, milk products, etc.

❊ If your compost is too wet, it will begin to smell. Turn it and mix in some dry material.

❊ If your compost is too dry, it won't decompose or "cook" fast enough. You can tell by taking the temperature of the pile. It should be warm to the touch in the early stages, hot while it's cooking, and warm again when it's ready to use. If there is not enough heat coming off the pile, sprinkle it down with the garden hose.

❊ Composting can also be slowed down by anything that sticks together, like a thick layer of leaves, and forms a barrier that keeps out air and moisture. Break the layer up or poke holes in it.

❊ Continue to add scraps to your pile in winter. Although the cooking process may slow down, or even stop in the coldest weather, the scraps break down especially quickly in the spring if they have been frozen.

❊ You shouldn't need to buy commercial compost accelerators if you follow the directions for proper composting. However, as a last resort, you might try this all-natural method: throw in a carton of fishing worms!

HOW IT'S DONE

The simplest way to compost is to dig a pit in an unused corner of your garden or yard. Toss in your kitchen scraps, cover with leaves or grass clippings and a little of the soil you dug out. Wood ashes from your fireplace and fur from your pet's brush make excellent periodic additions. Keep repeating the process. When you want to use the finished compost, dig it out from underneath.

Composting bins can be bought or built very inexpensively. Some municipalities also sell them for a reduced or subsidized rate. They should be about 1 yard (1 m) square and about 1 to 1 3/4 yards (1 to 1.5 m) high. The sides can be wood or a circle of snow or wire fencing. The bottom of the bin can be made of bricks and spaced 2-by-4s so that air circulates. There also needs to be an opening just above the bottom so you can scoop out the finished compost. The covering can be a wooden roof or something as simple as a ground sheet that can be anchored over your compost.

Balcony composting can be done in a variety of ways. *Mother Earth News* (No. 124) describes one of the easiest. You need two buckets or other waterproof containers, each big enough to hold about three weeks' worth of vegetable scraps, and about a bucketful of soil from a friend's garden. Each day, chop your leftover scraps into fine pieces, drain them if they are watery, and scatter them into bucket #1. Sprinkle some soil on top and stir well. Repeat the process each day. If your compost develops a nasty smell, it usually means it is not being aerated well enough. This could be caused by insufficient stirring or by waterlogging from inadequately drained scraps.

After about two weeks, switch to bucket #2. But still stir bucket #1 every day. In two more weeks, the compost in bucket #1 should be ready to use—it will look like thick, dark, crumbly soil. Feed it to your houseplants, windowboxes, or needy neighborhood trees and shrubs. Once you have enough, you can also use it instead of the garden soil for sprinkling into the compost bucket. Keep alternating buckets; you'll have a continuous supply of nutrients to give back to planet Earth! If you don't have a balcony you can even try this method right in the kitchen.

Detailed instructions for building a variety of compost bins are available in many magazines and books, such as *The Canadian Green Consumer Guide* and in free government brochures.

Books for More Information

The Canadian Green Consumer Guide. Pollution Probe. Revised edition. Toronto: McClelland & Stewart, 1991.

Nontoxic, Natural, and Earthwise. Debra Lynn Dadd. Los Angeles: Jeremy Tarcher, 1990.

The Nontoxic Home. Debra Lynn Dadd. Los Angeles: Jeremy Tarcher, 1986.

Heloise: Hints for a Healthy Planet. New York: Perigee Books, 1990.

CHAPTER SIX

RECIPES FOR
THE GREEN KITCHEN

These recipes have been contributed by well-known people who are concerned about the environment and by environmental activists who are known either individually or as part of a group for the fine work they are doing.

Marjorie Lamb's Granola

Almost all the dry ingredients (except the oats) in this recipe are optional. Also try adding rolled wheat, pumpkin seeds, or soy flakes. You might also try brewer's yeast—but be aware it has a very strong flavor.

4 cups	rolled oats	1 L
2 cups	wheat germ	500 mL
1 cup	shredded unsweetened coconut	250 mL
1 cup	shelled sunflower seeds	250 mL
1/3 cup	flax seeds	75 mL
1/2 cup	chopped nuts	125 mL
1/2 cup	skim milk powder	125 mL
1 cup plus 1 oz	safflower oil	250 mL plus 25 mL
1 1/4 cups	melted honey	300 mL
1 Tbsp	milk	15 mL
1 scant tsp	salt	5 mL
1 cup	raisins	250 mL

1. In a large bowl, mix together oats, wheat germ, coconut, sunflower seeds, flax seeds, nuts, and skim milk powder.
2. In a separate bowl, mix together oil, honey, milk, and salt.
3. Stir liquid ingredients into dry with a wooden spoon. Spread onto cookie sheets. Bake at 200° F (95° C) for 1 1/2 to 2 hours, stirring occasionally. Remove from oven and stir in raisins. Cool. Keeps for several weeks in airtight containers.

Marjorie Lamb is an environmental broadcaster and author of *Two Minutes a Day for a Greener Planet*.

Elizabeth Baird's Multigrain Cereal

Rolled oats can be substituted for the barley and whole wheat flakes, which, along with flax seeds, are available in bulk and health food stores.

1 1/3 cups	each rolled oats, barley flakes, and whole wheat flakes	325 mL
1 cup	raisins	250 mL
1/2 cup	unsalted sunflower seeds	125 mL
1/4 cup	flax seeds	50 mL
2 tsp	cinnamon	10 mL

1. In a large bowl, combine rolled oats, barley flakes, whole wheat flakes, raisins, sunflower seeds, flax seeds, and cinnamon.
2. Store in airtight container. Makes about 5 cups (1.25 L), enough for 15 servings.
3. For 1 serving: Combine 1/3 cup (75 mL) mix and 2/3 cup (150 mL) hot water. Microwave, uncovered, at High for 1 1/2 to 2 minutes or until desired consistency, stirring once. Let stand for 1 minute.

Elizabeth Baird is a food writer for *Canadian Living* magazine and the author of several cookbooks, including *Classic Canadian Cooking*.

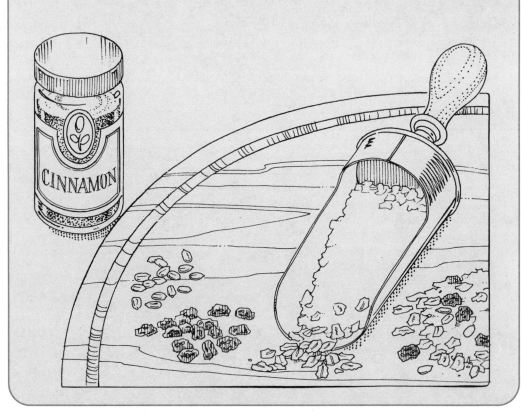

Robin's Zucchini Muffins

"This recipe was created with love for all of us gardeners who were a little too enthusiastic at planting time."

1 1/2 cups	flour	375 mL
1 cup	bran	250 mL
1 cup	brown sugar	250 mL
1 1/2 tsp	baking soda	7 mL
2 tsp	cinnamon	10 mL
1/3 cup	currants or raisins	75 mL
1/3 cup	dried apricots, diced	75 mL
1/3 cup	walnuts, crumbled	75 mL
2 cups	grated zucchini	500 mL
1/3 cup	applesauce	75 mL
3	eggs	3
3/4 cup	vegetable oil	175 mL
1 tsp	vanilla	5 mL

1. Mix together flour, bran, sugar, baking soda, and cinnamon. Add currants, apricots, nuts, and zucchini; stir well.
2. In a separate bowl, mix applesauce, eggs, oil, and vanilla.
3. Add liquid ingredients to dry ingredients; stir until just blended.
4. Spoon into greased muffin tins and bake at 375° F (190° C) for 15 to 20 minutes.

Makes 12 muffins.

Robin Edwards Davies is an environmentalist and enthusiastic organic gardener.

Green Kitchen Hint
Homemade baby food is good for baby and it saves you money. But all that cooking, puréeing, and blender washing is a lot of work for a few tablespoons of food. Solve the problem by cooking enough for several feedings at once. Freeze the extra puréed food in an ice-cube tray. As soon as the food is frozen, remove the cubes, wrap the baby-meal-size portions individually, and return them to the freezer.

Peter Mansbridge's Chicken Salad

A great summer recipe for people on the run.

3 cups	diced, cooked free-range chicken	750 mL
1 cup	chopped celery	250 mL
2 Tbsp	fresh-squeezed lemon juice	25 mL
1 cup	green grapes, halved	250 mL
1 cup	mandarin segments*	250 mL
1 cup	mayonnaise *or* low-fat mayonnaise *or* 1/2 cup (125 mL) each of mayonnaise and yogurt	
2 Tbsp	soy sauce *or* low-salt soy sauce	25 mL
	Toasted slivered almonds	

1. Combine all ingredients just before serving.
2. Serve with a tossed green salad, or on a bed of lettuce, with French bread.

Serves 4.

* If fruits such as mandarins do not grow in your area, you may want to substitute locally grown produce such as apples.

Peter Mansbridge is a national TV news anchor.

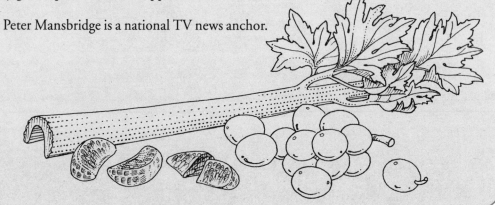

D.A. Chant's Zucchini Frittata

2 cups	grated zucchini	500 mL
	Butter or margarine	
1/2	green onion, chopped	1/2
1	clove garlic, chopped	1
1 cup	mushrooms, sliced	250 mL
1/2	red pepper, diced	1/2
5	eggs	5
1/2 cup	shredded Cheddar cheese	125 mL
	Chopped fresh parsley	
	Salt and black pepper	

1. Roll grated zucchini in tea towels and squeeze out moisture.
2. In large non-stick frypan, melt butter and sauté zucchini, onion, garlic, mushrooms, and red pepper for 5 to 8 minutes; remove from heat.
3. Lightly beat eggs in large bowl; stir in cheese, parsley, and pepper and salt to taste. Add sautéed vegetables and stir well.
4. Pour mixture into frypan. Cover and cook at medium heat for 10 minutes. Uncover and brown lightly under broiler. Slice into wedges and serve with steamed asparagus and a green salad.

Serves 4.

Dr. D.A. Chant is one of the founders of Pollution Probe.

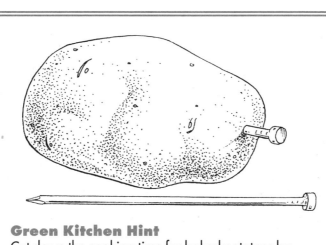

Green Kitchen Hint
Cut down the cooking time for baked potatoes by inserting long stainless steel nails lengthwise into each potato. The nails heat up the inside and can decrease cooking time by 25% to 50%.

Robert Bateman's Succotash and Crackers

2 cups	dried white navy beans	500 mL
5 cups	water	1.25 L
1	large onion	1
1	clove garlic	1
	Safflower oil	
Pinch	sage	Pinch
4 strips	bacon	4 strips
2	(14 oz/398 mL) cans cream-style corn	2
3 cups	skim milk	750 mL

1. Wash beans; cover with water and soak overnight. Rinse; put in a large saucepan with 5 cups (1.25 L) water. Cover, bring to a boil, and simmer until cooked.
2. Meanwhile, chop onion and garlic. Lightly fry in safflower oil until onion is pale golden. Sprinkle with a liberal pinch of sage; stir. Set aside.
3. In a frypan or microwave, cook bacon until crisp. Drain, break in pieces, and set aside.
4. When beans are cooked, add onion and garlic mixture and bacon. Stir in corn. Stir in milk. Bring to a boil; reduce heat and simmer, uncovered, for 10 minutes. Season with salt and pepper to taste.

Serves 4.

Crackers

1 cup	wheat bran	250 mL
1 cup	oat bran	250 mL
1 cup	rolled oats	250 mL
Pinch	salt	Pinch
	Additional oat bran for sprinkling	

1. Heat a dry saucepan over high heat. In a large bowl, stir together wheat bran, oat bran, rolled oats, and salt. Pour into hot pan; stir vigorously with a wooden spoon until mixture begins to smell toasty.
2. While continuing to stir, add sufficient hot water to make a fairly stiff porridge; the water will sizzle and boil. (If you wish, eat a little of this mixture as porridge.) Remove from heat. Sprinkle with additional oat bran until mixture is stiffer and "doughy."
3. Liberally sprinkle a non-stick cookie sheet with oat bran. Roll dough into small balls. Using wet fingers, flatten balls into thin wafers. Arrange close together on cookie sheet.
4. Set the cookie sheet atop a wood stove or in a very low oven (250° F/120° C) until crackers are dry and crisp and light brown.

Variation: Add 1/2 cup (125 mL) shredded aged or smoked cheese at porridge stage.

Robert Bateman is a world-renowned painter of wildlife.

Fiddlehead and Asparagus Stir-Fry

Use whatever quantities appeal to you.

Fiddleheads
Asparagus
Walnuts (halves or larger pieces)
Soy sauce
Lemon juice
Sesame oil
Oil for frying

1. Clean brown membranes from fiddleheads by washing, or by rubbing and winnowing surface-dried leaves. Trim asparagus and cut into 2-inch (5 cm) pieces.
2. Parboil fiddleheads for 3 minutes; drain. Heat oil in wok or heavy frypan. Fry fiddleheads for a minute or two; add asparagus and walnuts, and continue stirring until vegetables are in a yummy condition.
3. Season with soy sauce, lemon juice, and a dash of sesame oil. Serve immediately.

Variations: Add oyster sauce at the last moment, or add coarsely ground chilies during frying.

©1991 G. Michalenko

Dr. Greg Michalenko is with the Environment and Resource Studies Department at the University of Waterloo and is the author of a forthcoming cookbook.

Green Kitchen Hint
Save energy when cooking pasta on an electric stove. Bring salted water to a boil and stir in the pasta, cover the pot, turn off the heat, and let it stand for 15 minutes. Test for doneness, drain, and eat!

Mendelson Joe's "Broccoli Joe"

"People love my salads. The preparation time is five minutes and there's nothing so healthy as little trees (broccolis are little trees). Quantities are up to you."

2	fresh bulbous broccolis	2
	Raisins	
	Garlic cloves, chopped	
	Juice of 1 lemon	
	Soy sauce	
	Vegetable oil	
	Ground pepper	

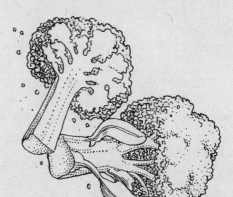

Options: Almonds
            Grated cheese
            Anchovies
            Black olives
            Chopped salami
            Chunks of orange
            Chunks of apple
            Dates
            Chopped ham

1. Wash and chop up broccoli flowerets. (Save the stalks for soup.)
2. In a salad bowl combine broccoli and raisins. Add the chopped garlic. Squeeze lemon juice over the little trees, then add the soy sauce.
3. Throw on a bit of vegetable oil and pepper, then toss the trees.
4. Then add whatever you want. Or add nothing!

Mendelson Joe is a multi-media artist-activist.

Green Kitchen Hint

Do you avoid cabbage—that inexpensive, locally grown standby—because of the all-pervasive smell it makes when cooking? Reduce the smell by placing a piece of bread or a slice of lemon in the cooking water. This also works for broccoli, and walnuts in the shell do the same when dropped into cauliflower cooking water.

Glen Loates's Caesar Salad

1	large head romaine lettuce	1
1/2 lb	lean bacon (optional)	250 g
6	egg yolks, well chilled*	6
2–3	cloves garlic, crushed	2–3
4	anchovy fillets, crushed	4
1/2 tsp	dry mustard	2 mL
1/2 tsp	Worcestershire sauce	2 mL
1/2 tsp	hot pepper sauce	2 mL
2 tsp	red wine vinegar	10 mL
1 cup	extra virgin olive oil	250 mL
	Freshly ground black pepper	
	Juice of 1/2 lemon	
3/4 cup	freshly grated	175 mL
plus 1–2 Tbsp	Parmesan cheese	plus 15–25 mL
	Freshly ground black pepper	
	Juice of 1/2 lemon	
	Croutons (recipe follows)	

1. Wash and dry lettuce leaves. Lay leaves on tea towels, roll up, and refrigerate until ready to use. In frypan or microwave, fry bacon (if using) until crisp; drain, break into small pieces, and set aside.

2. In a large wooden salad bowl, beat together vigorously with a wooden spoon the egg yolks, garlic, anchovies, dry mustard, Worcestershire sauce, hot pepper sauce, and red wine vinegar.

3. Put a few drops of oil on the countertop and place the salad bowl on them. Turn the bowl with one hand while, with the other hand, stirring the dressing with a wooden spoon. While continuing to spin and stir, add 1/2 cup (125 mL) oil a few drops at a time. (An assistant can pour a thin stream onto the inside edge of the bowl while you spin the bowl and stir.) Stir rapidly until the mixture is thick.

4. Add pepper to taste, juice of 1/2 lemon, and 1/2 cup (125 mL) Parmesan cheese. Beat well with wooden spoon. Add remaining 1/2 cup (125 mL) oil a little at a time while vigorously stirring the dressing, about 5 minutes. Stir in 1–2 Tbsp (15–25 mL) Parmesan cheese until dressing is desired consistency.

5. Tear lettuce into generous bite-sized pieces. Add to salad bowl with bacon and croutons; toss together lightly to coat with dressing. Sprinkle with remaining 1/4 cup (50 mL) Parmesan cheese, pepper to taste, and juice of remaining 1/2 lemon. Serve immediately.

To make croutons: Cut a French loaf into bite-sized cubes. Arrange on cookie sheet and bake at 250° F (120° C) until dry. Turn off oven; leave croutons in oven till ready to use.

Glen Loates is an acclaimed nature artist.

• Note: Please see the notes on the safety of raw eggs on page 91. If you choose to use raw eggs, make sure they have no cracks and have been washed thoroughly and kept continually chilled. Or 2 Tbsp oil and 1 Tbsp water can be substituted for each egg.

Quick and Juicy Tofu Burgers

2 slabs	organic tofu, cut into burger-size pieces	2 slabs
1/2 cup	low-salt tamari *or* other soy sauce	125 mL
1 Tbsp	lemon juice	15 mL
1/3 cup	virgin olive oil	75 mL
3–4	cloves garlic	3–4
3 Tbsp	tahini (optional: it thickens the sauce and boosts the protein) Freshly chopped herbs to taste	50 mL
1/4 tsp	cayenne	1 mL
1/3 cup	water	75 mL

1. Freeze tofu until solid; thaw in fridge or in microwave.
2. Combine remaining ingredients to make marinade. (If you want extra-juicy burgers, increase amount of olive oil.) Soak tofu in marinade for at least 1 hour, turning tofu regularly.
3. Barbecue (or cook in toaster oven) until burgers are golden brown, basting regularly with marinade. Serve on whole-wheat buns with condiments of your choice.

Serves 4.

Barry Kent MacKay is a writer and the director of Animal Alliance of Canada and of ZooCheck Canada.

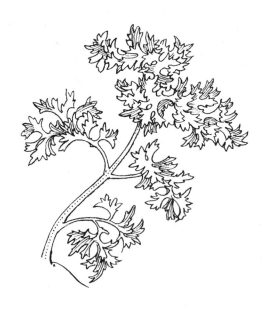

Green Kitchen Hint
Don't despair if you've added too much salt to a soup. Just throw in several slices of raw potato and cook for a while longer. Remove the potato before serving.

Michael O'Sullivan's Irish Cheese Cannelloni

Tastes best if you use all organically grown vegetables.

24	uncooked cannelloni shells	24
3 Tbsp	butter, cut in small pieces	50 mL
1	medium onion, chopped	1
3 Tbsp	all-purpose flour	50 mL
1 1/2 cups	apple juice	375 mL
1 cup	light cream	250 mL
1 1/4 cups	shredded Swiss cheese	300 mL
1/4 tsp	each salt and pepper	1 mL
1	bunch fresh spinach, chopped	1
1 1/2 cups	cottage cheese	375 mL
2/3 cup	ricotta cheese	150 mL
1/4 cup	freshly grated Parmesan cheese	50 mL
1 1/3 cups	chopped toasted almonds	325 mL
1	free-range egg, lightly beaten	1
1/4 tsp	nutmeg	1 mL
2	large tomatoes, chopped	2

1. In a large pot of boiling water, cook pasta until tender but firm; drain and rinse well under cold water. Drain again and set aside.

2. In a large bowl, mix together butter, onion, flour, apple juice, cream, Swiss cheese, and salt and pepper. Add spinach, cottage cheese, ricotta, Parmesan cheese, almonds, egg, and nutmeg. Blend well.

3. Stuff each cannelloni shell by hand. Arrange close together in shallow glass baking dish that has been lightly coated with vegetable oil. Sprinkle with chopped tomatoes. Cover with reusable aluminum foil. Bake at 350° F (180° C) for 35 minutes. Remove foil; broil for 3 minutes. Allow to cool slightly. Serve with fresh salad.

Serves 4.

Michael O'Sullivan is regional director for Canada and the North Pacific Rim of the World Society for the Protection of Animals.

Green Kitchen Hint

If you're making pasta for a dish that will require further cooking, for instance macaroni and cheese, decrease the original cooking time by one third, and complete the cooking in the oven.

Monte Hummel's Loon Lake Catfish

6	catfish (tofu is no substitute)	6
1 cup	breadcrumbs	250 mL
1 tsp	cayenne	5 mL
1 tsp	lemon pepper	5 mL
1	egg	1
	Dash of milk	
1	clove garlic, minced	1
	Olive oil for frying	

1. Buy an Ontario Fishing Licence, and check the regulations on whether the fish are fit to eat in your area.
2. Catch half a dozen fresh Ontario bullhead catfish, using worms near the bottom of the lake. Clean and skin the fish, remove heads but not the tails. (Put the rest out for the gulls.)
3. Combine breadcrumbs, cayenne, and lemon pepper.
4. Beat egg with a dash of milk and add the garlic.
5. Dip fish in egg mixture, then roll in breadcrumb mixture.
6. Sauté fish together in a spitting frypan of hot olive oil, about 4 to 5 minutes per side, until golden brown. Serve with fresh lemon, wild rice and wild mushrooms, steamed fiddleheads in June, and the best bottle of frosty Chardonnay you can afford (or cold beer!).

Serves 6.

Monte Hummel is president of World Wildlife Fund Canada and is one of the founders and a former executive director and chairman of Pollution Probe.

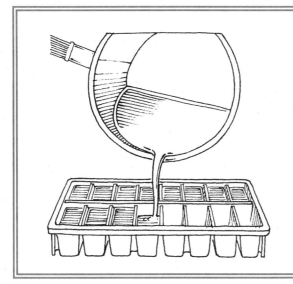

Green Kitchen Hint
Don't throw that vegetable cooking water away — even if it's only the small amount used in a steamer or pressure cooker. Pour it into an ice-cube tray, freeze, and store frozen cubes in a freezer bag. Thaw a few and use them as part of the water needed to cook rice, or use them in recipes calling for vegetable stock.

Janine Ferretti's Wild Rice Casserole or Stuffing

1 cup	wild rice	250 mL
3 Tbsp	butter	50 mL
1 cup	diced leek (white part only)	250 mL
1	large clove garlic, chopped	1
1/2 cup	chopped celery	125 mL
1 tsp	grated lemon rind	5 mL
1 Tbsp	freshly squeezed lemon juice	15 mL
	Salt and pepper to taste	
1 tsp	sage	5 mL
1 tsp	rosemary	5 mL
3 cups	white wine *or* 1 1/2 cups (375 mL) wine plus 1 1/2 cups (375 mL) water	750 mL
1 cup	currants	250 mL
2 Tbsp	chopped Italian parsley Freshly chopped parsley for garnish	25 mL

1. Wash wild rice well and drain.

2. Melt butter in large heavy saucepan over medium heat. Cook leek, garlic, and celery until just tender.

3. Add wild rice, lemon rind and juice, salt and pepper, sage, and rosemary; stir for 3 minutes.

4. Add wine or wine and water mixture and bring to boil. Reduce heat and simmer for 45 minutes or until liquid is absorbed. (You might have to remove the lid for the last few minutes.)

5. Butter a large casserole; add rice mixture, currants, and parsley. Mix well, cover tightly, and bake at 350° F (175° C) for 20 to 25 minutes or let the mixture cool and stuff a bird with it.

6. Sprinkle casserole with freshly chopped parsley and serve immediately.

Serves 4 to 6.

Janine Ferretti is the executive director of Pollution Probe.

Green Kitchen Hint
If you've burned your rice a little on the bottom, don't stir it. Add a heel from a loaf of fresh bread and leave it in the covered pot for a few minutes.

David Rains Wallace's Black Bean Soup

David Rains Wallace often helps his wife, Elizabeth Kendall, an artist and professional cook, prepare this dish. A perfect late-October California supper.

1 cup	dry black beans	250 mL
1 Tbsp	fruity olive oil	15 mL
3	bay leaves	3
4	long red mildly hot chilies	4
1 1/2	medium yellow onions, diced	1 1/2
1 Tbsp	olive oil	15 mL
2	cloves garlic, minced	2
2 tsp	oregano, crushed	10 mL
1/2 tsp	cumin	2 mL
1 Tbsp	sweet paprika	15 mL
1/2 cube	tomato bouillon *or* 1 Tbsp (15 mL) tomato paste *or* 1 peeled, seeded tomato, puréed	1/2 cube
1	lime, quartered	1
	Salt	

To prepare beans:
1. Wash and clean beans. Put them in a saucepan; fill with water to cover plus 1 inch (2.5 cm). Bring to a boil. Turn off heat and let sit 10 minutes or until beans are plump and smooth. Drain, and return to saucepan. Toss beans with 1 Tbsp (15 mL) olive oil.
2. Cover with fresh water. Add bay leaves. Bring very slowly to simmer over low flame, and simmer until beans are leather-hard—not crisp or dry but not soft. Remove from heat; leave in cooking liquid. Beans will absorb more moisture and flavor as they sit and can be prepared from several hours to 2 days in advance.

To prepare soup:
1. Dice chilies and onions; sauté in 1 Tbsp (15 mL) olive oil until tender. Add garlic, oregano, and cumin. As soon as garlic is clear, remove from heat; stir in paprika (paprika gets bitter if it gets dark).
2. Add pepper mixture to the beans; add water to bring to level of 6 cups (1.5 L).
3. Simmer until beans are tender. Stir in tomato bouillon and salt to taste. Squeeze lime over each serving.
Serve with corn tortillas, muffins, or bread and salad.

Serves 4.

David Rains Wallace writes eco-thrillers, among them *The Turquoise Dragon*.

Marla's Spaghetti Squash Casserole

This recipe is tastiest if it is made up in the morning and allowed to stand for several hours before baking.

1	8-inch spaghetti squash	1
1 cup	minced onion	250 mL
3	cloves garlic, minced	3
2	tomatoes, chopped	2
1/2 lb	mushrooms, quartered	250 g
1 cup	tomato sauce	250 mL
2 tsp	fresh oregano, chopped	10 mL
4 tsp	fresh basil, chopped	20 mL
4 tsp	fresh thyme, chopped	20 mL
1 1/2 cups	shredded mozzarella	375 mL
1/4 cup	fresh parsley, chopped	50 mL
1 cup	breadcrumbs	250 mL
	Freshly grated Parmesan cheese	

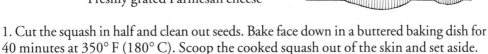

1. Cut the squash in half and clean out seeds. Bake face down in a buttered baking dish for 40 minutes at 350° F (180° C). Scoop the cooked squash out of the skin and set aside.
2. In a little oil, sauté onions and garlic in a large saucepan for about 1 minute; add tomatoes, mushrooms, tomato sauce, oregano, basil, and thyme. Add squash and mozzarella; toss together. Pour mixture into a buttered casserole. Top with parsley, breadcrumbs, and Parmesan cheese to taste. Bake at 350° F (180° C) for 45 minutes.

Serves 4.

Marla Allison, an environmental activist, is on the staff at Pollution Probe.

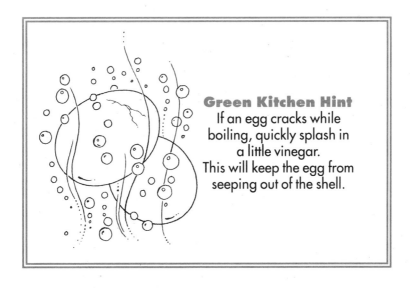

Green Kitchen Hint
If an egg cracks while boiling, quickly splash in a little vinegar.
This will keep the egg from seeping out of the shell.

Anton Kuerti's Artichokes alle mani

Many people have encountered artichokes only in an entirely defoliated state, preserved with chemicals, and wastefully packaged in bottles or cans. Yet eating freshly steamed artichokes—including a goodly portion of the commonly discarded leaves—is a gourmet delight.

Prepare 1 large or 2 small artichokes per person; you may wish to cut off a portion of the stem, and some people like to cut off about 1/2 inch (1 cm) from the tips of the leaves, which can be sharp. Steam for 6 to 8 minutes in a pressure cooker (or about 10 minutes in a microwave at High with 1 Tbsp/15 mL water). Serve with the following dipping sauce.

Sauce (serves 4)

1/3 cup plus 2 Tbsp	olive oil	100 mL
2 Tbsp	good quality vinegar	25 mL
	Juice of 1/4 lemon	
1 Tbsp	sesame tahini	15 mL
1/4 cup	grape, apple, or other fruit juice *or* sherry	50 mL
2 Tbsp	yogurt *or* sour cream	25 mL
1	clove garlic, crushed	1
1/2 tsp	salt *or* 2 tsp (10 mL) onion soup powder	2 mL
	Oregano, ground fennel, and/or thyme	
	Cornstarch to thicken	

1. In a small bowl, combine all ingredients, mixing with that wonderfully energy-efficient piece of kitchen equipment, the whisk. The consistency should be pourable but not so thin that the sauce will drip off the leaves: to thicken, add more cornstarch; to thin, add more fruit juice, lemon juice, or sherry. (Use any leftover sauce as a salad dressing.)

Anton Kuerti is a concert pianist and committed environmentalist.

Green Kitchen Hint

Have you ever wasted an egg by grabbing for one you thought was hard-boiled? Next time you're in doubt, spin the egg. A hard-boiled one spins smoothly, a raw one wobbles around.

Pierre Berton's Microwave Rhubarb Crisp

This standard recipe allows you to substitute or combine rhubarb with nuts, apples, strawberries, or whatever else you desire. Just keep the total amount of fruit constant.

2 cups	rhubarb	500 mL
2 Tbsp	lemon juice	25 mL
1 tsp	grated lemon rind	5 mL
1 Tbsp	grated orange rind	15 mL
1/2 cup	white sugar	125 mL
3/4 cup	all-purpose flour	175 mL
1 cup	rolled oats	250 mL
1 cup	brown sugar	250 mL
1/2 cup	soft butter or margarine	125 mL

1. Mix rhubarb, lemon juice and rind, orange rind, and white sugar; spread in a 9-inch (2.5 L) square glass baking dish.
2. Combine flour, rolled oats, brown sugar, and butter; mix until crumbly. Sprinkle on top of rhubarb.
3. Microwave, uncovered, for 15 minutes. Let stand for 5 minutes. Or bake in regular oven at 350° F (180° C) for approximately 45 minutes.
4. Serve hot or at room temperature.

Pierre Berton is an author, columnist, and commentator.

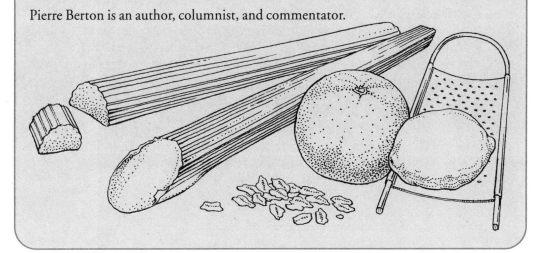

Green Kitchen Hint

Save energy when hard-boiling eggs on an electric stove: bring the eggs to a boil in a heavy, covered saucepan. Then turn off the heat and leave the eggs for about 20 minutes. They will be hard-cooked.

Stephen Best's Raisin Bread

"Bread making is a state of mind. You are dealing with living beings, yeast, who are about to do your bidding and, unbeknownst to them, die in your service. Give them due respect and understanding. To be successful, you must savor the process of making bread as much as you savor the bread itself."

1 tsp	sugar	5 mL
1 pkg	active dry yeast	1 pkg
1 Tbsp	salt	15 mL
2 Tbsp	sugar	25 mL
2 Tbsp	unsalted butter	25 mL
1 cup	cold milk	250 mL
2	eggs, lightly beaten	2
5–6 cups	whole-wheat flour	1.25–1.5 L
1 cup	bran	250 mL
2 cups	chopped raisins (Note: chop raisins with a wet knife)	500 mL

1. Fill a shallow pan with hot water and place it on the lowest rack in your oven; close the oven door. In a small, warmed bowl, dissolve 1 tsp (5 mL) sugar in 1/2 cup (125 mL) lukewarm water. What you have just prepared is a bowl of yeast feast. Sprinkle the yeast gently over the top of the sugar solution. Don't stir! The yeast will drown and die if you do. Cover the bowl with a cloth and set aside for 10 minutes.
2. Meanwhile, in a large, warmed mixing bowl, dissolve the salt, 2 Tbsp (25 mL) sugar, and butter in 1 cup (250 mL) boiling water. Stir in cold milk and the eggs. Mix in well 1 cup (250 mL) whole-wheat flour.
3. Stir the yeast mixture—which should have formed a nice head of foam—into the flour mixture. Add bran and mix well. Add raisins.
4. The next step is very important: the key to good bread is using the *least* amount of flour possible. Add 1 or 2 cups (250 to 500 mL) flour to the yeast mixture and stir with a large wooden spoon. Add flour 1/2 cup (125 mL) at a time until the dough is thick enough that you can no longer easily stir in the flour.

Green Kitchen Hint

After separating egg whites for use in a recipe,
you can cover the yolks
with cold water and store them in the fridge
for up to three days.

•

Egg whites can be frozen for a few months,
but remember to use twice as much once-frozen egg
white as fresh in your recipes.

5. Spread a thick layer of flour onto a clean, smooth, unmarred countertop. Dump the dough onto the flour (you may have to scrape the bowl to get all the dough out). Grease your hands with butter, cover the dough with a dusting of flour, and knead dough, occasionally adding flour, until dough no longer sticks to your hands. Stop adding flour, but continue to knead until the texture of the dough is consistent. Knead for another 5 minutes, at least. Fold the dough into a large ball.

6. Grease the inside of a warm bowl with butter. Put the dough in it, cover with a towel, and place in the oven with the pan of hot water. Leave the dough in the oven for 1 hour.

7. Take the dough out of the oven. Remove the pan of water, refill it with hot water, and return it to the oven. Dump the dough onto your kneading surface; grease your hands with butter. Punch down the dough until it is flat, fold it over into a ball, cover it with a fresh towel, and let it rest for 10 minutes.

8. Meanwhile, grease 2 bread pans with butter.

9. Knead the dough for at least 10 minutes, adding only enough flour to prevent the dough from seriously sticking. Divide dough into 2 portions. Knead each portion for another 5 minutes. Fold each portion into a loaf shape and place it in a bread pan. Pop the loaves into the oven with the pan of hot water; leave for 50 minutes.

10. Set the oven to 350° F (180° C). Do not open the oven door! Do not remove the pan of water! Bake the bread for 1 hour.

11. Remove the bread from the oven, pop the loaves out of the pans and place them, on their sides, on a rack; cover with a towel. (The cooking doesn't end when the bread is out of the oven.) Let them cool slowly on their sides. Once the bread is just warm to touch it is ready to eat. Raisin bread is best toasted and served with butter.

Makes 2 loaves.

Stephen Best is with the International Wildlife Coalition.

Green Kitchen Hint
Use stale bread for French toast — some chefs will use nothing else. It is also good for making stuffing, breadcrumbs, and croutons.

HAVING FUN WITH FOOD

While we're greening our kitchens, we need to keep sight of the fact that the kitchen is for preparing food — food that can meet our nutritional needs, delight our tastebuds, and introduce us to other cultures, or just be fun to prepare and eat. Here is a terrific recipe for baba ganouj, a great party food, and a few recipes that you and your kids will enjoy making and eating.

Roz's Baba Ganouj

This recipe is exceptionally good; it is different from traditional baba ganouj, which is creamier but not so light. For a more traditional recipe, use 1/2 cup (125 mL) tahini and only 2 Tbsp (25 mL) parsley.

2	medium eggplants, to yield 2 1/2 cups (625 mL) when cooked and mashed	2
1/2 cup	freshly squeezed lemon juice	125 mL
3 cups	finely chopped parsley	750 mL
4	green onions, finely chopped	4
3 Tbsp	tahini	50 mL
2	cloves garlic, finely minced	2
	Salt and pepper to taste	

1. Wash eggplants and prick them in several places with a fork.
2. Broil eggplants until the top is slightly charred (about 10 minutes). Turn a quarter turn. Repeat until all sides are charred. When done, the flesh should be soft but not mushy. Set aside to cool.
3. Slice eggplants in half and scoop the flesh out. Mash flesh with a potato masher.
4. Combine all ingredients. Serve with a selection of crackers and pita slices.

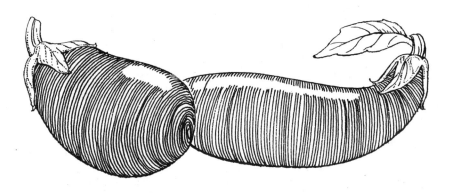

Quick Whole-Wheat Pizza

Dough

1 1/2 cups	whole-wheat flour	375 mL
1 cup	all-purpose flour	250 mL
1 cup	cornmeal	250 mL
2 tsp	baking powder	10 mL
1 tsp	baking soda	5 mL
1 tsp	salt	5 mL
1 1/2 cups	yogurt	375 mL
1/4 cup	canola oil	50 mL

1. In large bowl, combine dry ingredients. In a separate bowl, combine yogurt and oil; pour over flour mixture and stir with a fork to combine.
2. On lightly floured surface, knead dough lightly into ball. Cover and set aside. (Dough can be covered and refrigerated for up to 8 hours.)

Topping

2	cans (19 oz/540 mL) Italian Spice stewed tomatoes or regular stewed tomatoes plus 1/2 tsp (2 mL) basil	2
2 cups	broccoli florets	500 mL
1 cup	thinly sliced carrots	250 mL
1 1/2 cups	shredded low-fat mozzarella	375 mL
	Salt and pepper	
1	sweet green pepper, chopped	1
1/4 cup	freshly grated Parmesan cheese	50 mL

1. Drain tomatoes (reserve the juice for another use); chop, and return tomatoes to sieve. Set aside to drain.
2. Steam or boil broccoli and carrots until partially cooked but still crunchy. Drain, and refresh under cold water.

To prepare pizzas
1. With dampened hands, press dough into lightly greased 15- x 10-inch (2 L) jelly roll pan. Bake in 400° F (200° C) oven for 10 to 12 minutes or until firm.
2. Sprinkle half of the mozzarella over the crust. Spread tomatoes over cheese. Sprinkle with salt and pepper to taste. Top with broccoli, carrots, green pepper, remaining mozzarella, and Parmesan cheese.
3. Bake for 15 to 20 minutes or until bottom of crust is golden.

Serves 8.   Recipe courtesy *Canadian Living* magazine.

Fruit Leather Roll-ups

Your kids willl have a great time making and drying this money-saving, nutritious version of the heavily packaged, sugared, and preserved fruit leathers available in supermarkets. Almost any fruit can be used, but peaches, berries, and apples are traditional favorites. Three and a half cups (875 mL) chopped fresh fruit will yield 2 good-sized leathers.

	Fully-ripe fruit, cleaned, pitted, and finely chopped	
4 tsp	sugar or honey for each cup (250 mL) fruit	20 mL
	Vegetable oil	

1. In a saucepan, combine fruit and sweetening. Bring to boil, reduce heat, and simmer until fruit is just soft. Remove from heat and let cool.
2. Purée fruit in a blender or food mill, or force through a fine sieve.
3. Line cookie sheets with foil and grease the foil with vegetable oil.
4. Pour some of the puréed fruit into the middle of the foil and spread it out, leaving a 2-inch (5 cm) margin around the edges of the pan. The fruit spread should be about 1/4 inch (5 mm) thick.
5. Dry the fruit using a solar dryer as described in Chapter Four or by placing the cookie sheets in a gas oven with a pilot light for 6 to 8 hours. If neither of these environmental alternatives is available, you can try drying in your electric oven. Set the temperature for 130° F (55° C) for the first hour, raise it to 145° F (65° C) until the leathers are no longer tacky, and then lower the heat to 130° F (55° C) until nearly dry. Cool.
6. Properly dried leathers should be leathery and a little tough. Fold over the edges and roll the leathers up in the foil. Store in the fridge for up to 2 months or in the freezer for longer. Unroll carefully and use the foil again!

Pioneer Dandelion Salad

Gather young dandelion leaves, well before the flowers have begun to bloom. Be sure they are from a yard that has not been chemically treated in any way. Wash the leaves well, dry, and toss with an onion-and-vinegar salad dressing. Use wild onions if you can find them!

Halloween Pumpkin Seeds

Don't throw those pumpkin seeds away when you and your kids make jack-o'-lanterns. Add to the fun of Halloween by making these tasty snacks!

1. Remove the stringy insides and seeds from a small to medium pumpkin. Separate the seeds and spread them evenly on a cookie sheet. Salt or season as desired.
2. Place seeds in a 375° F (190° C) oven for about 15 minutes or until they begin popping.
3. Turn the seeds with a spatula and cook 5 minutes more or until the seeds pop rapidly.
4. Remove from oven, cool on the cookie sheet, and store in an airtight container.

CHAPTER SEVEN
THE KITCHEN AUDIT

Now that you've read *The Kitchen Handbook*, you can start—if you haven't already—making your kitchen (and your home, and—it's one small step—the earth) green.

We've summarized this book's major points in this section. Scan it now to see what you're doing right already, what you can start doing today, and what you can plan to do soon. Review the points frequently. Think of this as, in the short term, economizing and, in the long term, saving the planet.

CHAPTER ONE
GREENING THE KITCHEN

✳ Organize your kitchen to make recycling easy; set up a convenient recycling center nearby.

✳ Recycle as many of the containers, packaging materials, and papers and magazines as are accepted in your community's recycling program.

✳ Buy in bulk, and store bulk foods in large containers from which you can refill smaller, reusable containers to keep at hand in the kitchen.

✳ Whenever appropriate, consider switching from electric appliances to natural gas. (The same goes for home heating and water heating.)

✳ When you're shopping for an appliance, compare Energuide ratings.

✳ Use smaller, more energy-efficient appliances rather than larger ones (for example, a toaster oven or microwave instead of an oven; a slow cooker instead of a pot on a stovetop).

✳ Take good care of your kitchen appliances—keep them clean, read the instruction manuals, and use them properly —to maintain peak energy-efficiency.

✳ If you can use a hand-operated utensil instead of an electric appliance, *use it.*

✳ Practice water conservation in the kitchen:
   – Install aerators.
   – Fix leaky taps.
   – Use only as much water as you need.
   – Don't run water down the drain while you rinse dishes or clean vegetables.

✳ Install energy-efficient lighting—fluorescent instead of incandescent—and use task lighting rather than whole-room lighting.

✳ Check your dinnerware for lead content.

CHAPTER TWO
STOCKING YOUR SHELVES

✳ Choose locally grown produce.

✳ Choose in-season produce.

✳ Choose certified organic produce.

✳ If you can't find locally grown or organic produce where you shop, ask the produce manager to start stocking it.

✳ When you buy organic produce, make sure it's certified by a recognized agency.

✳ Find out what produce is grown in your state, province, or territory, and when in the year, so you can choose it instead of imported produce.

✳ Grow your own vegetables and herbs.

✳ Lobby the government and industry agencies to institute regulations requiring grocers to label waxed produce.

✳ Participate in or otherwise support seed banks and other programs designed to ensure seed diversity.

✳ Choose certified organic and free-range meat and animal products.

✳ When you're shopping, make unprocessed foods your first choice. Next choose those that are minimally processed (canned or frozen, for example). Avoid highly processed foods.

✳ Refuse to buy products that are unnecessarily or excessively packaged.

✳ Join a food buying club or food cooperative.

✳ Support alternative traders when you buy cash crops such as coffee and tea.

✳ Keep informed of boycotts, and support them.

CHAPTER THREE

USING THE GREEN KITCHEN

✳ Use your oven in the most energy-efficient way:
  – Cook several items in the oven at once.
  – Don't preheat the oven (except for baked goods).
  – Don't open the oven door while food is cooking.
  – Turn off the oven 10 to 15 minutes before the cooking time is up.

✳ Use your stovetop in the most energy-efficient way:
  – Use pots and pans with tight-fitting lids.

– Match the burner size to the bottom of the pan.

– Set the burner to the lowest temperature needed to cook the food.

✳ Use your refrigerator in the most energy-efficient way:

– Keep the temperature no lower than 37° F (3° C).

– Decide what you want to take out of the fridge before you open the door.

– Vacuum the coils at least twice a year.

✳ Use your freezer in the most energy-efficient way:

– Keep it about two-thirds full.

– Keep the temperature no lower than 0° F (–18° C).

– Freeze only as much food at one time as your unit can handle—about 3 lb per cu ft, or 5 kg per 100 L of capacity.

✳ Use energy-saving appliances such as pressure cookers and slow cookers as much as possible.

✳ Avoid putting in the microwave recycled paper, heat-susceptor or "brown and crisp" packaging, or any plastic not designed for microwave use.

✳ Eat *at least* one meatless main meal a week.

✳ Try to use meat as a supplement in a meal, rather than as the main ingredient.

CHAPTER FOUR

STORING AND PRESERVING FOODS

✳ Choose the freshest produce to reduce waste.

✳ Store fruits and vegetables properly to extend their life.

✳ Check the "best before" date before you buy something.

✳ To ensure that your bulk foods are fresh, buy them from a store that has a rapid turn-over.

✳ Buy only small quantities of foods you use only occasionally.

✳ To maximize food life:
  – Store eggs in the refrigerator.
  – Store cheese in tightly sealed containers.
  – Store legumes, grains (including flours and pastas), nuts, and seeds in tightly closed jars in a cool, dry place.
  – In humid summer months, store nuts, seeds, and whole-grain flours and pastas in the fridge.

✳ Buy large quantities of locally grown produce when it's in season and preserve it for later use by canning, freezing, drying, or placing in cool or cold storage.

✳ When you shop, go with a shopping list, and stick to it.

CHAPTER FIVE
KEEPING IT CLEAN AND GREEN

✳ Compost as much as you can.

✳ Make your own cleaners with vinegar, baking soda, pure soap, and cornstarch, instead of using commercial, toxic cleaners.

✳ Check before you buy that the label on the vinegar container specifies it's made from grain mash. If that isn't stated, the vinegar could be made from petroleum products.

✳ Clean up spills immediately to avoid having to use harsher cleaners—and more elbow grease—later.

✳ Keep your homemade cleaners in containers that are clearly labeled, unbreakable, and child-proof.

✳ Regularly descale (remove the mineral deposits from) appliances such as kettles and irons to keep them working efficiently.

✳ Use your dishwasher in the most energy-efficient way:
– Use it only when it's full.
– Use the short "econo" cycle.
– Let the dishes air dry instead of using the power dry cycle.

CHAPTER EIGHT
FOR MORE INFORMATION

GROUPS & ASSOCIATIONS

Advocacy Group for the Environmentally Sensitive ▲
1887 Chaine Court
Orleans, ON K1C 2W6

Agricultural Institute of Canada ♠ ✖
151 Slater Street, Suite 907
Ottawa, ON K1P 5H4

Alberta Pesticide Action Network ✖
10511 Saskatchewan Drive
Edmonton, AB T6H 4S1

Allergy and Environmental Health Association of Canada ♠ ✖
46 Highway - 8
Dundas, ON L9H 4V3

Back to the Farm Research Foundation ♠ ▲
Box 69
Davidson, SK S0G 1A0

BC Coalition for Alternatives to Pesticides ✖
RR 1, Mission Site
Sechelt, BC V0N 3A0

Canadian Animal Health Institute ◆
27 Cork Street West
Guelph, ON N1H 2W9

Canadian Animal Rights Network ◆
Box 687, Station Q
Toronto, ON M4T 2N5

Canadian Association of Chemical Distributors ✖
505 Consumers Road, Suite 607
Willowdale, ON M2J 4V8

Canadian Cattlemen's Association ♠
422 - 590 Keele Street
Toronto, ON M6N 3E3

Canadian Coalition to Stop Food Irradiation ▲
5262 Rumble Street, Suite 202
Burnaby, BC V5J 2B6

Canadian Council of Grocery Distributors ♠
475 - 750 Laurentien Boulevard
Montreal, PQ H4M 2M4

KEY	
Agriculture	♠
Animal Rights	◆
Health	▲
Pesticides	✖

Canadian Federation of Humane Societies ◆
30 Concourse Gate, 102
Nepean, ON K2E 7V7

Canadians for the Ethical Treatment of Food Animals ◆
Box 35597, Station E
Vancouver, BC V6M 4G9

Canadian Institute for Radiation Safety ▲
555 Richmond Street West, Suite 1106
Toronto, ON M5V 3B1

Canadian Organic Growers ♠
Box 6408, Station J
Ottawa, ON K2A 3Y6

Canadian Organic Producers Marketing Co-op ♠
Box 2000
Girvin, SK S0G 1X0

Centre for Sustainable Agriculture ♠ ✖
Box 9, Group 15
Hadashville, MB R0E 0X0

Citizens Against Neurotoxins ✖
154 Walnut Street
Winnipeg, MB R3G 1P1

City Farmer - Canada's Office of Urban Agriculture ♠
801 - 318 Homer Street
Vancouver, BC V6B 2V3

Concerned Parents Group ✖
Box 1021
Fredericton, NB E3B 5C4

Consumers' Health Organization of Canada ▲
Box 248
Willowdale, ON M2N 5S9

Crop Protection Institute of Canada ♠ ✖
21 Four Seasons Place, Suite 627
Etobicoke, ON M9B 6J8

EarthSave ♠ ▲
Box 7266
Oakville, ON L6J 6L6

Estrie contre l'irradiation ▲
1865, Mitchell
Lennoxville, PQ J1M 2A3

Friends of the Earth
251 Laurier Avenue West, Suite 701
Ottawa, ON K1P 5J6

Genetic Resources for Our World ♠
1132 Emperor Avenue
Ottawa, ON K1Z 8C1

Greenpeace - National
185 Spadina Avenue
Toronto, ON M5T 2C6

Grocery Products Manufacturers of Canada ♠
1185 Eglinton Avenue East, Suite 101
Don Mills, ON M3C 3C6

Groupe de travail sur les pesticides ✖
417, avenue Mont-Stephen
Westmount, PQ H3Y 2X7

Health Action Network Society ✖
202 - 5262 Rumble Street
Burnaby, BC V5J 2B6

Heritage Seed Program ♠
RR 3
Uxbridge, ON L0C 1K0

Jubilee Foundation for Agricultural Research ♠
115 Woolwich Street, 2nd Floor
Guelph, ON N1H 3V1

Mouvement pour l'agriculture biologique - région métropolitaine ♠
7638 Henri-Julien
Montreal, PQ H2R 2B5

Organic Crop Improvement Association ♠
RR 1
Walton, NS B0N 2R0

Parents of the Environmentally Sensitive ✖ ▲
Box 434, Station R
Toronto, ON M4G 4C3

People Against Chemical Sprays ✖
Box 393
Thunder Bay, ON P7C 4V9

Pesticide Education Network ✖
1369 Matheson Road
Gloucester, ON K1J 8B5

Pollution Probe
12 Madison Ave
Toronto, ON M5R 2S1

Preservation of Agricultural Lands Society - St. Catharines ♠
Box 1090
St. Catharines, ON L2R 7A3

Projet pour une agriculture écologique ♠
College MacDonald, CP 225
21 - 111 Lakeshore
Ste-Anne-de-Bellevue, PQ H9X 1C0

Regroupement protégéons notre santé et notre environnement ▲
18, rue Sainte-Marguerite ouest
Mercier, PQ J0L 1K0

Restorative Ecological Agriculture Project Society ♠
RR 1, Site 4, Box 30
St. Albert, AB T8N 1M8

Sustainable Agriculture Association ♠
10920 - 88th Avenue, Suite 103
Edmonton, AB T6G 0Z1

Sustainable Agriculture Movement ♠
492 Camden Place
Winnipeg, MB R3G 2V7

Women for the Survival of Agriculture ♠
RR 1
Metcalfe, ON K0C 2K0

World Society for the Protection of Animals ◆
55 University Avenue, Suite 902, Box 15
Toronto, ON M5J 2H7

Worldwide Home Environmentalists' Network ▲
1910 - 27th Street
West Vancouver, BC V7V 4L2

Zero Population Growth
Box 113
Ajax, ON L1S 3C5

NATIONAL AND REGIONAL
NETWORK OFFICES

Alberta Environmental Network
10511 Saskatchewan Drive
Edmonton, AB T6E 4S1

BC Environmental Network
2150 Maple Street
Vancouver, BC V6J 3T3

Canadian Environmental Network
Box 1289, Station B
Ottawa, Ontario K1P 5R3

Manitoba Eco-Network
Box 3125
Winnipeg, MB R3C 4E6

New Brunswick Environmental Network
Box 3006
Beresford, NB E0B 1H0

Newfoundland & Labrador Environmental Network
Box 11, Site 76
St. John's, NF A1C 5H4

Northern Environmental Network
Box 4163
Whitehorse, YT Y1A 3T3

Nova Scotia Environmental Network
RR2
North Sydney, NS B2A 3L8

Ontario Environmental Network
Park Mall
2 Quebec Street, Suite 201-C
Guelph, ON N1H 2T3

Prince Edward Island Envionmental Network
126 Richmond Street
Charlottetown, PE C1A 1H9

Réseau québécois des groupes écologistes
C.P. 1480, Succursale Place d'Armes
Montreal, PQ H2Y 3K8

Saskatchewan Eco-Network
219 - 22nd Street East, Suite 103
Saskatchewan, SK S7K 0G4

COOPERATIVES & TRADING COMPANIES

Bridgehead Distributing / Tools for Peace
9328 Jasper Avenue
Edmonton, AB T5H 3T5

Bridgehead Inc.
1011 Bloor Street West
Toronto, ON M6H 1M1

Bridgehead Inc.
20 James Street
Ottawa, ON K2P 0T6

Earth Harvest Cooperative
102 - 10th Street Northwest
Calgary, AB T2N 1V3

Harvest Collective
877 Westminster Avenue
Winnipeg, MB R3G 1B3

High Level Foods Co-op / Bridgehead Retailer
10313 - 82nd Avenue
Edmonton, AB T6E 1Z9

Ontario Federation of Food Cooperatives and Clubs
22 Mowat Avenue
Toronto, ON M6K 3E8

PSC Natural Foods
836 Viewfield Road
Victoria, BC V9A 4V1

Wild West Organic Harvest Co-op
East 2471 Simpson Road
Richmond, BC V5X 2R2

INTERNATIONAL

Arusha International Development Resource Centre
233 - 10th Street Northwest
Calgary, AB T2N 1V5

Canadian Council for International Cooperation
1 Nicholas Street, Suite 300
Ottawa, ON K1N 7B7

Canadian Hunger Foundation
323 Chapel Street
Ottawa, ON K1N 7B2

Canadian Physicians for Aid & Relief
64 Charles Street East
Toronto, On M4Y 1T1

CARE - Canada
1550 Carling Avenue
Box 9000
Ottawa, ON K1G 4X6

Friends of the Rainforest
Box 4612, Station E
Ottawa, ON K1S 5H8

Hope International Development Agency
210 - 6th Street
New Westminster, BC V3L 3A2

New Internationalist
1011 Bloor Street
Toronto, ON M6H 1M1

One Sky
136 Avenue F South
Saskatoon, SK S7M 1S8

Oxfam - Canada
251 Laurier Avenue West, Suite 301
Ottawa, ON K1P 5J6

Plenty Canada
RR 3
Lanark, ON K0G 1K0

Probe International
225 Brunswick Avenue
Toronto, ON M5S 2M6

SHAIR International Resource Centre
25 Hughson Street South, Suite 514
Hamilton, ON L8N 2A5

Stop 103 Inc.
Box 69, Station E
Toronto, ON M6H 4E1

Unicef Canada
443 Mount Pleasant Road
Toronto, ON M4S 2L8

Women & Environments Education & Development Foundation
736 Bathurst Street
Toronto, ON M5S 2R4

FEDERAL GOVERNMENT

Agriculture Canada
Ottawa, ON K1A 0C7

Environment Canada
Ottawa, ON K1A 0H3

Health & Welfare Canada
19th Floor, Jean Mance Bldg.
Ottawa, ON K1A 0K9

PROVINCIAL GOVERNMENTS

ALBERTA

Alberta Environment
Main Floor, 9820 - 106th Street
Edmonton, AB T5K 2J6

Alberta Health
7th Fl., Hys Centre, 11010 - 101st Street
Edmonton, AB T5J 2P4

Department of Agriculture
7000 - 113th Street
Edmonton, AB T6H 5T6

BRITISH COLUMBIA

Ministry of Agriculture and Fisheries
Parliament Bldgs.
Victoria, BC V8W 2Z7

Ministry of Environment
Parliament Bldgs.
Victoria, BC V8V 1X5

Ministry of Health
1515 Blanshard Street, Station 5-2
Victoria, BC V8W 3C8

MANITOBA

Department of Health
501 - 294 Portage Avenue
Winnipeg, MB R3G 0B9

Manitoba Agriculture
411 York Avenue
Winnipeg, MB R3C 3M1

Manitoba Environment
Box 7, Bldg. 2, 139 Tuxedo Avenue
Winnipeg, MB R3N 0H6

NEW BRUNSWICK
Department of Agriculture
Box 6000
Fredericton, NB E3B 5H1

Department of the Environment
Box 6000
Fredericton, NB E3B 5H1

Department of Health & Community Services
Box 5100
Fredericton, NB E3B 5G8

NEWFOUNDLAND
Department of Environment & Lands
Confederation Bldg., West Block
Box 8700
St. John's, NF A1B 4J6

Department of Forestry & Agriculture
Confederation Bldg., West Block
Box 8700
St. John's, NF A1B 4J6

Department of Health
Confederation Bldg., West Block
Box 8700
St. John's, NF A1B 4J6

NORTHWEST TERRITORIES
Department of Health
Yellowknife, NT X1A 2L9

Department of Renewable Resources
Yellowknife, NT X1A 2L9

NOVA SCOTIA
Department of Agriculture & Marketing
World Trade Convention Centre, Box 190
Halifax, NS B3J 2M4

Department of the Environment
Box 2107
Halifax, NS B3J 3B7

Department of Health & Fitness
Box 488, Joseph Howe Bldg.
Halifax, NS B3J 2R8

ONTARIO
Ministry of Agriculture & Food
Queen's Park
Toronto, ON M7A 2B2

Ministry of the Environment
135 St. Clair Avenue West
Toronto, ON M4V 1P5

Ministry of Health
9th Floor, Hepburn Block, Queen's Park
Toronto, ON M7A 1S2

PRINCE EDWARD ISLAND
Department of Agriculture
Box 2000
Charlottetown, PE C1A 7N8

Department of the Environment
Box 2000
Charlottetown, PE C1A 7N8

Department of Health & Social Services
Box 2000
Charlottetown, PE C1A 7N8

QUEBEC
Ministère de l'agriculture, des pêcheries et de l'alimentation
200A chemin Ste-Foy, 7e étage
Quebec, PQ G1R 4X6

Ministère de l'environnement
3900 rue Marly, Ste-Foy
Quebec, PQ G1X 4E4

Ministère de la santé et des services sociaux
1075 chemin Ste-Foy, 11e étage
Quebec, PQ G1S 2M1

SASKATCHEWAN
Department of the Environment & Public Safety
3085 Albert Street
Regina, SK S4S 0B1

Saskatchewan Agriculture and Foods
Walter Scott Bldg., 3085 Albert Street
Regina, SK S4S 0B1

Saskatchewan Health
3475 Albert Street
Regina, SK S4S 6X6

YUKON TERRITORY
Department of Health & Human Resources
Box 2703
Whitehorse, YT Y1A 2C6

INDEX

Food recipes are indicated by **bold face** type.

ABOUT POLLUTION PROBE
&
HOW YOU CAN HELP CLEAN UP MORE THAN JUST YOUR KITCHEN

Pollution Probe is one of Canada's most established, respected, and successful environmental groups. Since 1969, Pollution Probe has been working hard to educate and encourage children, adults, government, and business to adopt attitudes and behaviors that support a healthy environment.

As a non-profit organization, Pollution Probe relies heavily on contributions from individuals to keep its environmental research and education programs alive and effective.

You can help now by purchasing one or more beautiful Pollution Probe T-shirts for yourself, friends, and family.

- 100% unbleached cotton
- Six-colour graphic
- One size fits all
- Only $24.00 (including tax and shipping)

Yes, I want to help Pollution Probe clean and green our waters, air, and land. Please send me: _____ T-shirts at $24.00 each = $_____

Name _____

Address _____
              Number   Street

_____
              City   Province   Postal Code

Payment by: _____ Cheque _____ Visa _____ MasterCard

Credit Card # _____ Expiry Date _____

Mail to: Pollution Probe
             12 Madison Avenue
             Toronto, Ontario
             M5R 2S1
Or call: (416) 926-1907

Please allow four weeks for delivery.